THE SELECTED POEMS OF EZRA POUND

BY EZRA POUND

EZRA POUND

SELECTED POEMS

A New Directions Paperbook

TWENTY-SECOND PRINTING

CONTENTS

v

vii

BIOGRAPHY

E.P.

Born, Hailey, Idaho, 30 Oct. 1885.
Educ. U. of Penn. and Hamilton. PhB. '05. M.A. '06.

Published. 1908. Venice; A Lume Spento.

1909, Mathews, London. Personae, Exultations.
Thereafter some 40 volumes, in London till 1920.
N. York 1920–'30.
1930 onwards, with Faber, London, and in U.S.

1918 began investigation of causes of war, to oppose same. Lectured in the Università Bocconi, Milan, 1931, on Jefferson and Van Buren.

From 1932 continual polemic in two languages, moving from Social Credit to Gesellism.

Obtaining imprint in Italy of Social Credit and Gesellite doctrines, comparing them with Catholic canonist theory and local practice.

1939 first visit to U.S. since 1910 in endeavour to stave off war. D.Litt, honorary, from Hamilton.

1940 after continued opposition obtained permission to use Rome radio for personal propaganda in support of U.S. Constitution, continuing after America's official entry into the war only on condition that he should never be asked to say anything contrary to his conscience or contrary to his duties as an American Citizen. Which promise was faithfully observed by the Italian Government.

E.P. (1949)

CINO

Italian Campagna 1309, *the open road*

Bah! I have sung women in three cities,
But it is all the same;
And I will sing of the sun.

Lips, words, and you snare them,
Dreams, words, and they are as jewels,
Strange spells of old deity,
Ravens, nights, allurement:
And they are not;
Having become the souls of song.

Eyes, dreams, lips, and the night goes.
Being upon the road once more,
They are not.
Forgetful in their towers of our tuneing
Once for wind-runeing
They dream us-toward and
Sighing, say, "Would Cino,
Passionate Cino, of the wrinkling eyes,
Gay Cino, of quick laughter,
Cino, of the dare, the jibe.
Frail Cino, strongest of his tribe
That tramp old ways beneath the sun-light,
Would Cino of the Luth were here!"

Once, twice, a year—
Vaguely thus word they:

"Cino?" "Oh, eh, Cino Polnesi
The singer is't you mean?"

"Ah yes, passed once our way,
A saucy fellow, but . . .
(Oh they are all one these vagabonds),
Peste! 'tis his own songs?
Or some other's that he sings?
But *you*, My Lord, how with your city?"

But you "My Lord," God's pity!
And all I knew were out, My Lord, you
Were Lack-land Cino, e'en as I am,
O Sinistro.

I have sung women in three cities.
But it is all one.
I will sing of the sun.
. . . eh? . . . they mostly had grey eyes,
But it is all one, I will sing of the sun.

" 'Pollo Phoibee, old tin pan, you
Glory to Zeus' aegis-day,
Shield o' steel-blue, th' heaven o'er us
Hath for boss thy lustre gay!

'Pollo Phoibee, to our way-fare
Make thy laugh our wander-lied;
Bid thy 'fulgence bear away care.
Cloud and rain-tears pass they fleet!

Seeking e'er the new-laid rast-way
To the gardens of the sun . . .

.   .   .   .   .

I have sung women in three cities
But it is all one.

2

I will sing of the white birds
In the blue waters of heaven,
The clouds that are spray to its sea."

NA AUDIART

Que be-m vols mal

NOTE: Anyone who has read anything of the troubadours knows
well the tale of Bertran of Born and My Lady Maent of Mon-
tagnac, and knows also the song he made when she would none
of him, the song wherein he, seeking to find or make her equal,
begs of each preëminent lady of Langue d'Oc some trait or some
fair semblance: thus of Cembelins her "esgart amoros" to wit,
her love-lit glance, of Aelis her speech free-running, of the Vicom-
tess of Chalais her throat and her two hands, at Roacoart of Anhes
her hair golden as Iseult's; and even in this fashion of Lady Audiart
"although she would that ill come unto him" he sought and praised
the lineaments of the torse. And all this to make "Una dompna
soiseubuda" a borrowed lady or as the Italians translated it "Una
donna ideale."

Though thou well dost wish me ill
                    Audiart, Audiart,
Where thy bodice laces start
As ivy fingers clutching through
Its crevices,
                    Audiart, Audiart,
Stately, tall and lovely tender
Who shall render
                    Audiart, Audiart,
Praises meet unto thy fashion?
Here a word kiss!
                    Pass I on
Unto Lady "Miels-de-Ben,"

3

Having praised thy girdle's scope
How the stays ply back from it;
I breathe no hope
That thou shouldst . . .
                    Nay no whit
Bespeak thyself for anything.
Just a word in thy praise, girl,
Just for the swirl
Thy satins make upon the stair,
'Cause never a flaw was there
Where thy torse and limbs are met
Though thou hate me, read it set
In rose and gold.[1]
Or when the minstrel, tale half told,
Shall burst to lilting at the praise
                    "Audiart, Audiart" . . .
Bertrans, master of his lays,
Bertrans of Aultaforte thy praise
Sets forth, and though thou hate me well,
Yea though thou wish me ill,
                    Audiart, Audiart.
Thy loveliness is here writ till,
                    Audiart,
Oh, till thou come again.[2]
And being bent and wrinkled, in a form
That hath no perfect limning, when the warm
Youth dew is cold
Upon thy hands, and thy old soul
Scorning a new, wry'd casement,
Churlish at seemed misplacement,

[1] *I.e.*, in illumed manuscript.
[2] Reincarnate.

4

Finds the earth as bitter
As now seems it sweet,
Being so young and fair
As then only in dreams,
Being then young and wry'd,
Broken of ancient pride,
Thou shalt then soften,
Knowing, I know not how,
Thou wert once she
                    Audiart, Audiart
For whose fairness one forgave
                    Audiart,
Audiart
         Que be-m vols mal.

VILLONAUD FOR THIS YULE

Towards the Noel that morte saison
(*Christ make the shepherds' homage dear!*)
Then when the grey wolves everychone
Drink of the winds their chill small-beer
And lap o' the snows food's gueredon
Then makyth my heart his yule-tide cheer
(Skoal! with the dregs if the clear be gone!)
Wining the ghosts of yester-year.

Ask ye what ghosts I dream upon?
(*What of the magians' scented gear?*)
The ghosts of dead loves everyone
That make the stark winds reek with fear

5

Lest love return with the foison sun
And slay the memories that me cheer
(Such as I drink to mine fashion)
Wining the ghosts of yester-year.

Where are the joys my heart had won?
(*Saturn and Mars to Zeus drawn near!*) [1]
Where are the lips mine lay upon,
Aye! where are the glances feat and clear
That bade my heart his valour don?
I skoal to the eyes as grey-blown mere
(Who knows whose was that paragon?)
Wining the ghosts of yester-year.

Prince: ask me not what I have done
Nor what God hath that can me cheer
But ye ask first where the winds be gone
Wining the ghosts of yester-year.

THE TREE

I stood still and was a tree amid the wood,
Knowing the truth of things unseen before;
Of Daphne and the laurel bough
And that god-feasting couple old
That grew elm-oak amid the wold.
'Twas not until the gods had been
Kindly entreated, and been brought within
Unto the hearth of their heart's home

[1] *Signum Nativitatis.*

6

That they might do this wonder thing;
Nathless I have been a tree amid the wood
And many a new thing understood
That was rank folly to my head before.

THE WHITE STAG

I ha' seen them 'mid the clouds on the heather.
Lo! they pause not for love nor for sorrow,
Yet their eyes are as the eyes of a maid to her lover,
When the white hart breaks his cover
And the white wind breaks the morn.
    "'Tis the white stag, Fame, we're a-hunting,
    Bid the world's hounds come to horn!"

SESTINA: ALTAFORTE

LOQUITUR: *En* Bertrans de Born. Dante Alighieri put this man in hell
for that he was a stirrer up of strife. Eccovi! Judge ye! Have I dug
him up again? The scene is at his castle, Altaforte. "Papiols" is his
jongleur. "The Leopard," the *device* of Richard Cœur de Lion.

I

Damn it all! all this our South stinks peace.
You whoreson dog, Papiols, come! Let's to music!
I have no life save when the swords clash.
But ah! when I see the standards gold, vair, purple, opposing
And the broad fields beneath them turn crimson,
Then howl I my heart nigh mad with rejoicing.

II

In hot summer have I great rejoicing
When the tempests kill the earth's foul peace,
And the lightnings from black heav'n flash crimson,
And the fierce thunders roar me their music
And the winds shriek through the clouds mad, opposing,
And through all the riven skies God's swords clash.

III

Hell grant soon we hear again the swords clash!
And the shrill neighs of destriers in battle rejoicing,
Spiked breast to spiked breast opposing!
Better one hour's stour than a year's peace
With fat boards, bawds, wine and frail music!
Bah! there's no wine like the blood's crimson!

IV

And I love to see the sun rise blood-crimson.
And I watch his spears through the dark clash
And it fills all my heart with rejoicing
And pries wide my mouth with fast music
When I see him so scorn and defy peace,
His lone might 'gainst all darkness opposing.

V

The man who fears war and squats opposing
My words for stour, hath no blood of crimson

8

But is fit only to rot in womanish peace
Far from where worth's won and the swords clash
For the death of such sluts I go rejoicing;
Yea, I fill all the air with my music.

VI

Papiols, Papiols, to the music!
There's no sound like to swords swords opposing,
No cry like the battle's rejoicing
When our elbows and swords drip the crimson
And our charges 'gainst "The Leopard's" rush clash.
May God damn for ever all who cry "Peace!"

VII

And let the music of the swords make them crimson!
Hell grant soon we hear again the swords clash!
Hell blot black for alway the thought "Peace!"

BALLAD OF THE GOODLY FERE

Simon Zelotes speaking after the Crucifixion. Fere = Mate, Companion.

Ha' we lost the goodliest fere o' all
For the priests and the gallows tree?
Aye lover he was of brawny men,
O' ships and the open sea.

When they came wi' a host to take Our Man
His smile was good to see,
"First let these go!" quo' our Goodly Fere,
"Or I'll see ye damned," says he.

Aye he sent us out through the crossed high spears
And the scorn of his laugh rang free,
"Why took ye not me when I walked about
Alone in the town?" says he.

Oh we drank his "Hale" in the good red wine
When we last made company,
No capon priest was the Goodly Fere
But a man o' men was he.

I ha' seen him drive a hundred men
Wi' a bundle o' cords swung free,
That they took the high and holy house
For their pawn and treasury.

They'll no' get him a' in a book I think
Though they write it cunningly;
No mouse of the scrolls was the Goodly Fere
But aye loved the open sea.

If they think they ha' snared our Goodly Fere
They are fools to the last degree.
"I'll go to the feast," quo' our Goodly Fere,
"Though I go to the gallows tree."

"Ye ha' seen me heal the lame and blind,
And wake the dead," says he,

"Ye shall see one thing to master all:
'Tis how a brave man dies on the tree."

A son of God was the Goodly Fere
That bade us his brothers be.
I ha' seen him cow a thousand men.
I have seen him upon the tree.

He cried no cry when they drave the nails
And the blood gushed hot and free,
The hounds of the crimson sky gave tongue
But never a cry cried he.

I ha' seen him cow a thousand men
On the hills o' Galilee,
They whined as he walked out calm between,
Wi' his eyes like the grey o' the sea,

Like the sea that brooks no voyaging
With the winds unleashed and free,
Like the sea that he cowed at Genseret
Wi' twey words spoke' suddenly.

A master of men was the Goodly Fere,
A mate of the wind and sea,
If they think they ha' slain our Goodly Fere
They are fools eternally.

I ha' seen him eat o' the honey-comb
Sin' they nailed him to the tree.

PLANH FOR THE YOUNG ENGLISH KING

That is, Prince Henry Plantagenet, elder brother to Richard Cœur de Lion.

If all the grief and woe and bitterness,
All dolour, ill and every evil chance
That ever came upon this grieving world
Were set together they would seem but light
Against the death of the young English King.
Worth lieth riven and Youth dolorous,
The world o'ershadowed, soiled and overcast,
Void of all joy and full of ire and sadness.

Grieving and sad and full of bitterness
Are left in teen the liegemen courteous,
The joglars supple and the troubadours.
O'er much hath ta'en Sir Death that deadly warrior
In taking from them the young English King,
Who made the freest hand seem covetous.
'Las! Never was nor will be in this world
The balance for this loss in ire and sadness!

O skillful Death and full of bitterness,
Well mayst thou boast that thou the best chevalier
That any folk e'er had, hast from us taken;
Sith nothing is that unto worth pertaineth
But had its life in the young English King
And better were it, should God grant his pleasure,
That he should live than many a living dastard
That doth but wound the good to ire and sadness.

From this faint world, how full of bitterness
Love takes his way and holds his joy deceitful,

12

Sith no thing is but turneth unto anguish
And each to-day 'vails less than yestere'en,
Let each man visage this young English King
That was most valiant 'mid all worthiest men!
Gone is his body fine and amorous,
Whence have we grief, discord and deepest sadness.

Him, whom it pleased for our great bitterness
To come to earth to draw us from misventure,
Who drank of death for our salvacioun,
Him do we pray as to a Lord most righteous
And humble eke, that the young English King
He please to pardon, as true pardon is,
And bid go in with honourèd companions
There where there is no grief, nor shall be sadness.

From the Provençal of Bertrans de Born "Si tuit li dolh elh plor elh marrimen."

"BLANDULA, TENELLA, VAGULA"

What hast thou, O my soul, with paradise?
Will we not rather, when our freedom's won,
Get us to some clear place wherein the sun
Lets drift in on us through the olive leaves
A liquid glory? If at Sirmio,
My soul, I meet thee, when this life's outrun,
Will we not find some headland consecrated
By aery apostles of terrene delight,
Will not our cult be founded on the waves,
Clear sapphire, cobalt, cyanine,

13

On triune azures, the impalpable
Mirrors unstill of the eternal change?

Soul, if She meet us there, will any rumour
Of havens more high and courts desirable
Lure us beyond the cloudy peak of Riva?

ERAT HORA

"Thank you, whatever comes." And then she turned
And, as the ray of sun on hanging flowers
Fades when the wind hath lifted them aside,
Went swiftly from me. Nay, whatever comes
One hour was sunlit and the most high gods
May not make boast of any better thing
Than to have watched that hour as it passed.

THE HOUSE OF SPLENDOUR

'Tis Evanoe's,
A house not made with hands,
But out somewhere beyond the worldly ways
Her gold is spread, above, around, inwoven;
Strange ways and walls are fashioned out of it.

And I have seen my Lady in the sun,
Her hair was spread about, a sheaf of wings,
And red the sunlight was, behind it all.

And I have seen her there within her house,
With six great sapphires hung along the wall,
Low, panel-shaped, a-level with her knees,
And all her robe was woven of pale gold.

There are there many rooms and all of gold,
Of woven walls deep patterned, of email,
Of beaten work; and through the claret stone,
Set to some weaving, comes the aureate light.

Here am I come perforce my love of her,
Behold mine adoration
Maketh me clear, and there are powers in this
Which, played on by the virtues of her soul,
Break down the four-square walls of standing time.

THE TOMB AT AKR ÇAAR

"I am thy soul, Nikoptis. I have watched
These five millenia, and thy dead eyes
Moved not, nor ever answer my desire,
And thy light limbs, wherethrough I leapt aflame,
Burn not with me nor any saffron thing.

See, the light grass sprang up to pillow thee,
And kissed thee with a myriad grassy tongues;
But not thou me.
I have read out the gold upon the wall,
And wearied out my thought upon the signs.
And there is no new thing in all this place.

I have been kind. See, I have left the jars sealed,
Lest thou shouldst wake and whimper for thy wine.
And all thy robes I have kept smooth on thee.

O thou unmindful! How should I forget!
—Even the river many days ago,
The river? thou wast over young.
And three souls came upon Thee—
And I came.
And I flowed in upon thee, beat them off;
I have been intimate with thee, known thy ways.
Have I not touched thy palms and finger-tips,
Flowed in, and through thee and about thy heels?
How 'came I in'? Was I not thee and Thee?

And no sun comes to rest me in this place,
And I am torn against the jagged dark,
And no light beats upon me, and you say
No word, day after day.

Oh! I could get me out, despite the marks
And all their crafty work upon the door,
Out through the glass-green fields. . . .

* * * *

Yet it is quiet here:
I do not go."

PORTRAIT D'UNE FEMME

Your mind and you are our Sargasso Sea,
London has swept about you this score years

16

And bright ships left you this or that in fee:
Ideas, old gossip, oddments of all things,
Strange spars of knowledge and dimmed wares of price.
Great minds have sought you—lacking someone else.
You have been second always. Tragical?
No. You preferred it to the usual thing:
One dull man, dulling and uxorious,
One average mind—with one thought less, each year.
Oh, you are patient, I have seen you sit
Hours, where something might have floated up.
And now you pay one. Yes, you richly pay.
You are a person of some interest, one comes to you
And takes strange gain away:
Trophies fished up; some curious suggestion;
Fact that leads nowhere; and a tale or two,
Pregnant with mandrakes, or with something else
That might prove useful and yet never proves,
That never fits a corner or shows use,
Or finds its hour upon the loom of days:
The tarnished, gaudy, wonderful old work;
Idols and ambergris and rare inlays,
These are your riches, your great store; and yet
For all this sea-hoard of deciduous things,
Strange woods half sodden, and new brighter stuff:
In the slow float of different light and deep,
No! there is nothing! In the whole and all,
Nothing that's quite your own.
                    Yet this is you.

AN OBJECT

This thing, that hath a code and not a core,
Hath set acquaintance where might be affections,
And nothing now
       Disturbeth his reflections.

THE SEAFARER

From the Anglo-Saxon

May I, for my own self, song's truth reckon,
Journey's jargon, how I in harsh days
Hardship endured oft.
Bitter breast-cares have I abided,
Known on my keel many a care's hold,
And dire sea-surge, and there I oft spent
Narrow nightwatch nigh the ship's head
While she tossed close to cliffs. Coldly afflicted,
My feet were by frost benumbed.
Chill its chains are; chafing sighs
Hew my heart round and hunger begot
Mere-weary mood. Lest man know not
That he on dry land loveliest liveth,
List how I, care-wretched, on ice-cold sea,
Weathered the winter, wretched outcast
Deprived of my kinsmen;
Hung with hard ice-flakes, where hail-scur flew,
There I heard naught save the harsh sea
And ice-cold wave, at whiles the swan cries,
Did for my games the gannet's clamour,
Sea-fowls' loudness was for me laughter,

The mews' singing all my mead-drink.
Storms, on the stone-cliffs beaten, fell on the stern
In icy feathers; full oft the eagle screamed
With spray on his pinion.
                                        Not any protector
May make merry man faring needy.
This he little believes, who aye in winsome life
Abides 'mid burghers some heavy business,
Wealthy and wine-flushed, how I weary oft
Must bide above brine.
Neareth nightshade, snoweth from north,
Frost froze the land, hail fell on earth then,
Corn of the coldest. Nathless there knocketh now
The heart's thought that I on high streams
The salt-wavy tumult traverse alone.
Moaneth alway my mind's lust
That I fare forth, that I afar hence
Seek out a foreign fastness.
For this there's no mood-lofty man over earth's midst,
Not though he be given his good, but will have in his youth
        greed;
Nor his deed to the daring, nor his king to the faithful
But shall have his sorrow for sea-fare
Whatever his lord will.
He hath not heart for harping, nor in ring-having
Nor winsomeness to wife, nor world's delight
Nor any whit else save the wave's slash,
Yet longing comes upon him to fare forth on the water.
Bosque taketh blossom, cometh beauty of berries,
Fields to fairness, land fares brisker,
All this admonisheth man eager of mood,
The heart turns to travel so that he then thinks

On flood-ways to be far departing.
Cuckoo calleth with gloomy crying,
He singeth summerward, bodeth sorrow,
The bitter heart's blood. Burgher knows not—
He the prosperous man—what some perform
Where wandering them widest draweth.
So that but now my heart burst from my breastlock,
My mood 'mid the mere-flood,
Over the whale's acre, would wander wide.
On earth's shelter cometh oft to me,
Eager and ready, the crying lone-flyer,
Whets for the whale-path the heart irresistibly,
O'er tracks of ocean; seeing that anyhow
My lord deems to me this dead life
On loan and on land, I believe not
That any earth-weal eternal standeth
Save there be somewhat calamitous
That, ere a man's tide go, turn it to twain.
Disease or oldness or sword-hate
Beats out the breath from doom-gripped body.
And for this, every earl whatever, for those speaking after—
Laud of the living, boasteth some last word,
That he will work ere he pass onward,
Frame on the fair earth 'gainst foes his malice,
Daring ado, . . .
So that all men shall honour him after
And his laud beyond them remain 'mid the English,
Aye, for ever, a lasting life's-blast,
Delight 'mid the doughty.
                              Days little durable,
And all arrogance of earthen riches,
There come now no kings nor Cæsars

Nor gold-giving lords like those gone.
Howe'er in mirth most magnified,
Whoe'er lived in life most lordliest,
Drear all this excellence, delights undurable!
Waneth the watch, but the world holdeth.
Tomb hideth trouble. The blade is layed low.
Earthly glory ageth and seareth.
No man at all going the earth's gait,
But age fares against him, his face paleth,
Grey-haired he groaneth, knows gone companions,
Lordly men, are to earth o'ergiven,
Nor may he then the flesh-cover, whose life ceaseth,
Nor eat the sweet nor feel the sorry,
Nor stir hand nor think in mid heart,
And though he strew the grave with gold,
His born brothers, their buried bodies
Be an unlikely treasure hoard.

Δώρια

Be in me as the eternal moods
        of the bleak wind, and not
As transient things are—
        gaiety of flowers.
Have me in the strong loneliness
        of sunless cliffs
And of grey waters.
        Let the gods speak softly of us
In days hereafter,
        The shadowy flowers of Orcus
Remember thee.

APPARUIT

Golden rose the house, in the portal I saw
thee, a marvel, carven in subtle stuff, a
portent. Life died down in the lamp and flickered,
            caught at the wonder.

Crimson, frosty with dew, the roses bend where
thou afar, moving in the glamorous sun,
drinkst in life of earth, of the air, the tissue
            golden about thee.

Green the ways, the breath of the fields is thine there,
open lies the land, yet the steely going
darkly hast thou dared and the dreaded æther
            parted before thee.

Swift at courage thou in the shell of gold, cast-
ing a-loose the cloak of the body, camest
straight, then shone thine oriel and the stunned light
            faded about thee.

Half the carven shoulder, the throat aflash with
strands of light inwoven about it, loveli-
est of all things, frail alabaster, ah me!
            swift in departing.

Clothed in goldish weft, delicately perfect,
gone as wind! The cloth of the magical hands!
Thou a slight thing, thou in access of cunning
            dar'dst to assume this?

A VIRGINAL

No, no! Go from me. I have left her lately.
I will not spoil my sheath with lesser brightness,
For my surrounding air hath a new lightness;
Slight are her arms, yet they have bound me straitly
And left me cloaked as with a gauze of æther;
As with sweet leaves; as with subtle clearness.
Oh, I have picked up magic in her nearness
To sheathe me half in half the things that sheathe her.
No, no! Go from me. I have still the flavour,
Soft as spring wind that's come from birchen bowers.
Green come the shoots, aye April in the branches,
As winter's wound with her sleight hand she staunches,
Hath of the trees a likeness of the savour:
As white their bark, so white this lady's hours.

OF JACOPO DEL SELLAIO

This man knew out the secret ways of love,
No man could paint such things who did not know.
And now she's gone, who was his Cyprian,
And you are here, who are "The Isles" to me.

And here's the thing that lasts the whole thing out:
The eyes of this dead lady speak to me.

THE RETURN

See, they return; ah, see the tentative
Movements, and the slow feet,
The trouble in the pace and the uncertain
Wavering!

See, they return, one, and by one,
With fear, as half-awakened;
As if the snow should hesitate
And murmur in the wind,
             and half turn back;
These were the "Wing'd-with-Awe,"
             Inviolable,

Gods of the wingèd shoe!
With them the silver hounds,
             sniffing the trace of air!

Haie! Haie!
        These were the swift to harry;
These the keen-scented;
These were the souls of blood.

Slow on the leash,
             pallid the leash-men!

TENZONE

Will people accept them?
    (i.e. these songs).

24

As a timorous wench from a centaur
        (or a centurion),
Already they flee, howling in terror.

Will they be touched with the verisimilitudes?
        Their virgin stupidity is untemptable.
I beg you, my friendly critics,
Do not set about to procure me an audience.

I mate with my free kind upon the crags;
        the hidden recesses
Have heard the echo of my heels,
        in the cool light,
        in the darkness.

THE GARRET

Come, let us pity those who are better off than we are.
Come, my friend, and remember
        that the rich have butlers and no friends,
And we have friends and no butlers.
Come, let us pity the married and the unmarried.

Dawn enters with little feet
        like a gilded Pavlova,
And I am near my desire.
Nor has life in it aught better
Than this hour of clear coolness,
        the hour of waking together.

25

THE GARDEN

En robe de parade.

Samain

Like a skein of loose silk blown against a wall
She walks by the railing of a path in Kensington Gardens,
And she is dying piece-meal
       of a sort of emotional anæmia.

And round about there is a rabble
Of the filthy, sturdy, unkillable infants of the very poor.
They shall inherit the earth.

In her is the end of breeding.
Her boredom is exquisite and excessive.
She would like some one to speak to her,
And is almost afraid that I
       will commit that indiscretion.

SALUTATION

O generation of the thoroughly smug
      and thoroughly uncomfortable,
I have seen fishermen picnicking in the sun,
I have seen them with untidy families,
I have seen their smiles full of teeth
      and heard ungainly laughter.
And I am happier than you are,
And they were happier than I am;
And the fish swim in the lake
      and do not even own clothing.

THE SPRING

'Ἦρι μὲν αἴ τε κυδώνιαι—Ibycus

Cydonian Spring with her attendant train,
Maelids and water-girls,
Stepping beneath a boisterous wind from Thrace,
Throughout this sylvan place
Spreads the bright tips,
And every vine-stock is
Clad in new brilliancies.

                  And wild desire
Falls like black lightning.
O bewildered heart,
Though every branch have back what last year lost,
She, who moved here amid the cyclamen,
Moves only now a clinging tenuous ghost.

A PACT

I make a pact with you, Walt Whitman—
I have detested you long enough.
I come to you as a grown child
Who has had a pig-headed father;
I am old enough now to make friends.
It was you that broke the new wood,
Now is a time for carving.
We have one sap and one root—
Let there be commerce between us.

DANCE FIGURE

For the Marriage in Cana of Galilee

Dark eyed,
O woman of my dreams,
Ivory sandaled,
There is none like thee among the dancers,
None with swift feet.

I have not found thee in the tents,
In the broken darkness.
I have not found thee at the well-head
Among the women with pitchers.

Thine arms are as a young sapling under the bark;
Thy face as a river with lights.

White as an almond are thy shoulders;
As new almonds stripped from the husk.
They guard thee not with eunuchs;
Not with bars of copper.

Gilt turquoise and silver are in the place of thy rest.
A brown robe, with threads of gold woven in patterns, hast
    thou gathered about thee,
O Nathat-Ikanaie, "Tree-at-the-river."

As a rillet among the sedge are thy hands upon me;
Thy fingers a frosted stream.

Thy maidens are white like pebbles;
Their music about thee!

28

There is none like thee among the dancers;
None with swift feet.

APRIL

Nympharum membra disjecta

Three spirits came to me
And drew me apart
To where the olive boughs
Lay stripped upon the ground:
Pale carnage beneath bright mist.

THE REST

O helpless few in my country,
O remnant enslaved!

Artists broken against her,
A-stray, lost in the villages,
Mistrusted, spoken-against,

Lovers of beauty, starved,
Thwarted with systems,
Helpless against the control;

You who can not wear yourselves out
By persisting to successes,
You who can only speak,
Who can not steel yourselves into reiteration;

You of the finer sense,
Broken against false knowledge,
You who can know at first hand,
Hated, shut in, mistrusted:

Take thought:
I have weathered the storm,
I have beaten out my exile.

LES MILLWIN

The little Millwins attend the Russian Ballet.
The mauve and greenish souls of the little Millwins
Were seen lying along the upper seats
Like so many unused boas.

The turbulent and undisciplined host of art students—
The rigorous deputation from "Slade"—
Was before them.

With arms exalted, with fore-arms
Crossed in great futuristic X's, the art students
Exulted, they beheld the splendours of *Cleopatra*.

And the little Millwins beheld these things;
With their large and anæmic eyes they looked out upon this
    configuration.

Let us therefore mention the fact,
For it seems to us worthy of record.

A SONG OF THE DEGREES

I

Rest me with Chinese colours,
For I think the glass is evil.

II

The wind moves above the wheat—
With a silver crashing,
A thin war of metal.

I have known the golden disc,
I have seen it melting above me.
I have known the stone-bright place,
        The hall of clear colours.

III

O glass subtly evil, O confusion of colours!
O light bound and bent in, O soul of the captive,
Why am I warned? Why am I sent away?
Why is your glitter full of curious mistrust?
O glass subtle and cunning, O powdery gold!
O filaments of amber, two-faced iridescence!

ITÉ

Go, my songs, seek your praise from the young and from the
    intolerant,

Move among the lovers of perfection alone.
Seek ever to stand in the hard Sophoclean light
And take your wounds from it gladly.

SALVATIONISTS

I

Come, my songs, let us speak of perfection—
We shall get ourselves rather disliked.

II

Ah yes, my songs, let us resurrect
The very excellent term *Rusticus*.
Let us apply it in all its opprobrium
To those to whom it applies.
And you may decline to make them immortal,
For we shall consider them and their state
In delicate
Opulent silence.

III

Come, my songs,
Let us take arms against this sea of stupidities—
Beginning with Mumpodorus;
And against this sea of vulgarities—
Beginning with Nimmim;
And against this sea of imbeciles—
All the Bulmenian literati.

ARIDES

The bashful Arides
Has married an ugly wife,
He was bored with his manner of life,
Indifferent and discouraged he thought he might as
Well do this as anything else.

Saying within his heart, "I am no use to myself,
"Let her, if she wants me, take me."
He went to his doom.

AMITIES

Old friends the most.—W. B. Y.

I

To one, on returning certain years after.

You wore the same quite correct clothing,
You took no pleasure at all in my triumphs,
You had the same old air of condescension
Mingled with a curious fear
        That I, myself, might have enjoyed them.
Te Voilà, mon Bourrienne, you also shall be immortal.

II

To another.

And we say good-bye to you also,
For you seem never to have discovered

That your relationship is wholly parasitic;
Yet to our feasts you bring neither
Wit, nor good spirits, nor the pleasing attitudes
        Of discipleship.

III

But you, *bos amic*, we keep on,
For to you we owe a real debt:
In spite of your obvious flaws,
You once discovered a moderate chop-house.

MEDITATIO

When I carefully consider the curious habits of dogs
I am compelled to conclude
That man is the superior animal.

When I consider the curious habits of man
I confess, my friend, I am puzzled.

CODA

O My songs,
Why do you look so eagerly and so curiously into people's
        faces,
Will you find your lost dead among them?

THE COMING OF WAR: ACTAEON

An image of Lethe,
    and the fields
Full of faint light
    but golden,
Gray cliffs,
    and beneath them
A sea
Harsher than granite,
    unstill, never ceasing;
High forms
    with the movement of gods,
Perilous aspect;
    And one said:
"This is Actaeon."
    Actaeon of golden greaves!
Over fair meadows,
Over the cool face of that field,
Unstill, ever moving
Hosts of an ancient people,
The silent cortège.

IN A STATION OF THE METRO

The apparition of these faces in the crowd;
Petals on a wet, black bough.

ALBA

As cool as the pale wet leaves
                    of lily-of-the-valley
She lay beside me in the dawn.

COITUS

The gilded phaloi of the crocuses
                    are thrusting at the spring air.
Here is there naught of dead gods
But a procession of festival,
A procession, O Giulio Romano,
Fit for your spirit to dwell in.
Dione, your nights are upon us.

The dew is upon the leaf.
The night about us is restless.

THE ENCOUNTER

All the while they were talking the new morality
Her eyes explored me.
And when I arose to go
Her fingers were like the tissue
Of a Japanese paper napkin.

'IMÉPPΩ

Thy soul
Grown delicate with satieties,
Atthis.
O Atthis,
I long for thy lips.
I long for thy narrow breasts,
Thou restless, ungathered.

TAME CAT

"It rests me to be among beautiful women.
Why should one always lie about such matters?
I repeat:
It rests me to converse with beautiful women
Even though we talk nothing but nonsense,

The purring of the invisible antennæ
Is both stimulating and delightful."

THE TEA SHOP

The girl in the tea shop
        Is not so beautiful as she was,
The August has worn against her.
She does not get up the stairs so eagerly;
Yes, she also will turn middle-aged,

37

And the glow of youth that she spread about us
     As she brought us our muffins
Will be spread about us no longer.
     She also will turn middle-aged.

ANCIENT MUSIC

Winter is icummen in,
Lhude sing Goddamm,
Raineth drop and staineth slop,
And how the wind doth ramm!
     Sing: Goddamm.
Skiddeth bus and sloppeth us,
An ague hath my ham.
Freezeth river, turneth liver,
     Damn you, sing: Goddamm.
Goddamm, Goddamm, 'tis why I am, Goddamm,
     So 'gainst the winter's balm.
Sing goddamm, damm, sing Goddamm.
Sing goddamm, sing goddamm, DAMM.

NOTE: This is not folk music, but Dr. Ker writes that the tune is to be found under the Latin words of a very ancient canon.

THE LAKE ISLE

O God, O Venus, O Mercury, patron of thieves,
Give me in due time, I beseech you, a little tobacco-shop,
With the little bright boxes
     piled up neatly upon the shelves

38

And the loose fragrant cavendish
        and the shag,
And the bright Virginia
        loose under the bright glass cases,
And a pair of scales not too greasy,
And the whores dropping in for a word or two in passing,
For a flip word, and to tidy their hair a bit.

O God, O Venus, O Mercury, patron of thieves,
Lend me a little tobacco-shop,
        or install me in any profession
Save this damn'd profession of writing,
        where one needs one's brains all the time.

EPITAPHS

Fu I

Fu I loved the high cloud and the hill,
Alas, he died of alcohol.

Lı Po

And Li Po also died drunk.
He tried to embrace a moon
In the Yellow River.

VILLANELLE: THE PSYCHOLOGICAL HOUR

I had over-prepared the event,
        that much was ominous.

With middle-ageing care
        I had laid out just the right books.
I had almost turned down the pages.

        Beauty is so rare a thing.
        So few drink of my fountain.

So much barren regret,
So many hours wasted!
And now I watch, from the window,
        the rain, the wandering busses.

"Their little cosmos is shaken"—
        the air is alive with that fact.
In their parts of the city
        they are played on by diverse forces.
How do I know?
        Oh, I know well enough.
For them there is something afoot.
        As for me;
I had over-prepared the event—

        Beauty is so rare a thing,
        So few drink of my fountain.

Two friends: a breath of the forest . . .
Friends? Are people less friends
        because one has just, at last, found them?
Twice they promised to come.

        "Between the night and morning?"

Beauty would drink of my mind.
Youth would awhile forget
                my youth is gone from me.

II

("Speak up! You have danced so stiffly?
        Someone admired your works,
        And said so frankly.

        "Did you talk like a fool,
        The first night?
        The second evening?"

"*But* they promised again:
                'To-morrow at tea-time.' ")

III

Now the third day is here—
                no word from either;
No word from her nor him,
Only another man's note:
                "Dear Pound, I am leaving England."

PAGANI'S, NOVEMBER 8

Suddenly discovering in the eyes of the very beautiful
                Normande cocotte
The eyes of the very learned British Museum assistant.

ALBA

from "Langue d'Oc"

When the nightingale to his mate
Sings day-long and night late
My love and I keep state
In bower,
In flower,
'Till the watchman on the tower
Cry:

> "Up! Thou rascal, Rise,
> I see the white
> > Light
> > And the night
> > > Flies."

NEAR PERIGORD

> *A Perigord pres del muralh*
> *Tan que i puosch' om gitar ab malh.*

You'd have men's hearts up from the dust
And tell their secrets, Messire Cino,
Right enough? Then read between the lines of Uc St. Circ,
Solve me the riddle, for you know the tale.

Bertrans, En Bertrans, left a fine canzone:
"Maent, I love you, you have turned me out.
The voice at Montfort, Lady Agnes' hair,
Bel Miral's stature, the viscountess' throat,

42

Set all together, are not worthy of you. . . ."
And all the while you sing out that canzone,
Think you that Maent lived at Montaignac,
One at Chalais, another at Malemort
Hard over Brive—for every lady a castle,
Each place strong.

                    Oh, *is* it easy enough?
Tairiran held hall in Montagnac,
His brother-in-law was all there was of power
In Perigord, and this good union
Gobbled all the land, and held it later for some hundred years.
And our En Bertrans was in Altafort,
Hub of the wheel, the stirrer-up of strife,
As caught by Dante in the last wallow of hell—
The headless trunk "that made its head a lamp,"
For separation wrought out separation,
And he who set the strife between brother and brother
And had his way with the old English king,
Viced in such torture for the "counterpass."

How would you live, with neighbours set about you—
Poictiers and Brive, untaken Rochecouart,
Spread like the finger-tips of one frail hand;
And you on that great mountain of a palm—
Not a neat ledge, not Foix between its streams,
But one huge back half-covered up with pine,
Worked for and snatched from the string-purse of Born—
The four round towers, four brothers—mostly fools:
What could he do but play the desperate chess,
And stir old grudges?

"Pawn your castles, lords!
Let the Jews pay."
            And the great scene—
(That, maybe, never happened!)
            Beaten at last,
Before the hard old king:
            "Your son, ah, since he died
"My wit and worth are cobwebs brushed aside
"In the full flare of grief. Do what you will."

Take the whole man, and ravel out the story.
He loved this lady in castle Montagnac?
The castle flanked him—he had need of it.
You read to-day, how long the overlords of Perigord,
The Talleyrand, have held the place; it was no transient fiction.
And Maent failed him? Or saw through the scheme?

      And all his net-like thought of new alliance?
Chalais is high, a-level with the poplars.
Its lowest stones just meet the valley tips
Where the low Dronne is filled with water-lilies.
And Rochecouart can match it, stronger yet,
The very spur's end, built on sheerest cliff,
And Malemort keeps its close hold on Brive,
While Born, his own close purse, his rabbit warren,
His subterranean chamber with a dozen doors,
A-bristle with antennæ to feel roads,
To sniff the traffic into Perigord.
And that hard phalanx, that unbroken line,
The ten good miles from there to Maent's castle,

44

All of his flank—how could he do without her?
And all the road to Cahors, to Toulouse?
What would he do without her?

 "Papiol,
Go forthright singing—Anhes, Cembelins.
There is a throat; ah, there are two white hands;
There is a trellis full of early roses,
And all my heart is bound about with love.
Where am I come with compound flatteries—
What doors are open to fine compliment?"
And every one half jealous of Maent?
He wrote the catch to pit their jealousies
Against her; give her pride in them?

Take his own speech, make what you will of it—
And still the knot, the first knot, of Maent?

 Is it a love poem? Did he sing of war?
Is it an intrigue to run subtly out,
Born of a jongleur's tongue, freely to pass
Up and about and in and out the land,
Mark him a craftsman and a strategist?
(St. Leider had done as much as Polhonac,
Singing a different stave, as closely hidden.)
Oh, there is precedent, legal tradition,
To sing one thing when your song means another,
"Et albirar ab lor bordon—"
Foix' count knew that. What is Sir Bertrans' singing?
Maent, Maent, and yet again Maent,
Or war and broken heaumes and politics?

II

End fact. Try fiction. Let us say we see
En Bertrans, a tower-room at Hautefort,
Sunset, the ribbon-like road lies, in red cross-light,
Southward toward Montaignac, and he bends at a table
Scribbling, swearing between his teeth; by his left hand
Lie little strips of parchment covered over,
Scratched and erased with *al* and *ochaisos*.
Testing his list of rhymes, a lean man? Bilious?
With a red straggling beard?
And the green cat's-eye lifts toward Montagnac.

Or take his "magnet" singer setting out,
Dodging his way past Aubeterre, singing at Chalais
    In the vaulted hall,
Or, by a lichened tree at Rochecouart
Aimlessly watching a hawk above the valleys,
Waiting his turn in the mid-summer evening,
Thinking of Aelis, whom he loved heart and soul . . .
To find her half alone, Montfort away,
And a brown, placid, hated woman visiting her,
Spoiling his visit, with a year before the next one.
Little enough?
Or carry him forward. "Go through all the courts,
My Magnet," Bertrans had said.

We came to Ventadour
In the mid love court, he sings out the canzon,
No one hears save Arrimon Luc D'Esparo—
No one hears aught save the gracious sound of compliments
Sir Arrimon counts on his fingers, Montfort,

Rochecouart, Chalais, the rest, the tactic,
Malemort, guesses beneath, sends word to Cœur-de-Lion:
The compact, de Born smoked out, trees felled
About his castle, cattle driven out!
Or no one sees it, and En Bertrans prospered?

    And ten years after, or twenty, as you will,
Arnaut and Richard lodge beneath Chalus:
The dull round towers encroaching on the field,
The tents tight drawn, horses at tether
Further and out of reach, the purple night,
The crackling of small fires, the bannerets,
The lazy leopards on the largest banner,
Stray gleams on hanging mail, an armourer's torch-flare
Melting on steel.

    And in the quietest space
They probe old scandals, say de Born is dead;
And we've the gossip (skipped six hundred years).
Richard shall die to-morrow—leave him there
Talking of *trobar clus* with Daniel.
And the "best craftsman" sings out his friend's song,
Envies its vigour . . . and deplores the technique,
Dispraises his own skill?—That's as you will.
And they discuss the dead man.
Plantagenet puts the riddle: "Did he love her?"
And Arnaut parries: "Did he love your sister?
True, he has praised her, but in some opinion
He wrote that praise only to show he had
The favour of your party; had been well received."

"You knew the man."
      "*You* knew the man."

"I am an artist, you have tried both métiers."
"You were born near him."
                    "Do we know our friends?"
"Say that he saw the castles, say that he loved Maent!"
"Say that he loved her, does it solve the riddle?"
    End the discussion, Richard goes out next day
And gets a quarrel-bolt shot through his vizard,
Pardons the bowman, dies,

                    Ends our discussion. Arnaut ends
"In sacred odour"—(that's apocryphal!)
And we can leave the talk till Dante writes:
Surely I saw, and still before my eyes
Goes on that headless trunk, that bears for light
Its own head swinging, gripped by the dead hair,
And like a swinging lamp that says, "Ah me!
I severed men, my head and heart
Ye see here severed, my life's counterpart."

Or take En Bertrans?

III

> *Ed eran due in uno, ed uno in due;*
> Inferno, XXVIII, 125

Bewildering spring, and by the Auvezere
Poppies and day's eyes in the green émail
Rose over us; and we knew all that stream,
And our two horses had traced out the valleys;
Knew the low flooded lands squared out with poplars,
In the young days when the deep sky befriended.
    And great wings beat above us in the twilight,
48

And the great wheels in heaven
Bore us together . . . surging . . . and apart . . .
Believing we should meet with lips and hands,

    High, high and sure . . . and then the counterthrust:
'Why do you love me? Will you always love me?
But I am like the grass, I can not love you.'
Or, 'Love, and I love and love you,
And hate your mind, not *you*, your soul, your hands.'

        So to this last estrangement, Tairiran!

        There shut up in his castle, Tairiran's,
She who had nor ears nor tongue save in her hands,
Gone—ah, gone—untouched, unreachable!
She who could never live save through one person,
She who could never speak save to one person,
And all the rest of her a shifting change,
A broken bundle of mirrors . . . !

SONG OF THE BOWMEN OF SHU

Here we are, picking the first fern-shoots
And saying: When shall we get back to our country?
Here we are because we have the Ken-in for our foemen,
We have no comfort because of these Mongols.
We grub the soft fern-shoots,
When anyone says "Return," the others are full of sorrow.
Sorrowful minds, sorrow is strong, we are hungry and thirsty.
Our defence is not yet made sure, no one can let his friend re-
    turn.
We grub the old fern-stalks.

We say: Will we be let to go back in October?
There is no ease in royal affairs, we have no comfort.
Our sorrow is bitter, but we would not return to our country.
What flower has come into blossom?
Whose chariot? The General's.
Horses, his horses even, are tired. They were strong.
We have no rest, three battles a month.
By heaven, his horses are tired.
The generals are on them, the soldiers are by them.
The horses are well trained, the generals have ivory arrows
    and quivers ornamented with fish-skin.
The enemy is swift, we must be careful.
When we set out, the willows were drooping with spring,
We come back in the snow,
We go slowly, we are hungry and thirsty,
Our mind is full of sorrow, who will know of our grief?

Shih-ching (Odes), 127

THE BEAUTIFUL TOILET

Blue, blue is the grass about the river
And the willows have overfilled the close garden.
And within, the mistress, in the midmost of her youth,
White, white of face, hesitates, passing the door.
Slender, she puts forth a slender hand;

And she was a courtezan in the old days,
And she has married a sot,
Who now goes drunkenly out
And leaves her too much alone.

Attributed to Mei Shêng, 140 B.C.
50

THE RIVER SONG

This boat is of satō-wood, and its gunwhales are cut magnolia,
Musicians with jewelled flutes and with pipes of gold
Fill full the sides in rows, and our wine
Is rich for a thousand cups.
We carry singing girls, drift with the drifting water,
Yet Sennin needs
A yellow stork for a charger, and all our seamen
Would follow the white gulls or ride them.
Kutsu's prose song
Hangs with the sun and moon.

King So's terraced palace
           is now but barren hill,
But I draw pen on this barge
Causing the five peaks to tremble,
And I have joy in these words
           like the joy of blue islands.
(If glory could last forever
Then the waters of Han would flow northward.)
     *   *   *   *

And I have moped in the Emperor's garden, awaiting an order-
    to-write!
I looked at the dragon-pond, with its willow-coloured water
Just reflecting the sky's tinge,
And heard the five-score nightingales aimlessly singing.

The eastern wind brings the green colour into the island
    grasses at Ei-shū,
The purple house and the crimson are full of Spring softness.
South of the pond the willow-tips are half-blue and bluer,

Their cords tangle in mist, against the brocade-like palace.
Vine-strings a hundred feet long hang down from carved rail-
    ings,
And high over the willows, the fine birds sing to each other,
    and listen,
Crying—"Ken-Kwan," for the early wind, and the feel of it.
The wind bundles itself into a bluish cloud and wanders off
Over a thousand gates, over a thousand doors are the sounds of
    spring singing,
And the Emperor is at Kō.
Five clouds hang aloft, bright on the purple sky,
The imperial guards come forth from the golden house with
    their armour a-gleaming.
The Emperor in his jewelled car goes out to inspect his
    flowers,
He goes out to Hōrai, to look at the wing-flapping storks,
He returns by way of Shi rock, to hear the new nightingales,
For the gardens at Jō-rin are full of new nightingales,
Their sound is mixed in this flute,
Their voice is in the twelve pipes here.

By Rihaku (Li T'ai Po), 8th century A.D.

THE RIVER-MERCHANT'S WIFE: A LETTER

While my hair was still cut straight across my forehead
I played about the front gate, pulling flowers.
You came by on bamboo stilts, playing horse,
You walked about my seat, playing with blue plums.
And we went on living in the village of Chōkan:
Two small people, without dislike or suspicion.

52

At fourteen I married My Lord you.
I never laughed, being bashful.
Lowering my head, I looked at the wall.
Called to, a thousand times, I never looked back.

At fifteen I stopped scowling,
I desired my dust to be mingled with yours
Forever and forever and forever.
Why should I climb the look out?

At sixteen you departed,
You went into far Ku-tō-en, by the river of swirling eddies,
And you have been gone five months.
The monkeys make sorrowful noise overhead.

You dragged your feet when you went out.
By the gate now, the moss is grown, the different mosses,
Too deep to clear them away!
The leaves fall early this autumn, in wind.
The paired butterflies are already yellow with August
Over the grass in the West garden;
They hurt me. I grow older.
If you are coming down through the narrows of the river
    Kiang,
Please let me know beforehand,
And I will come out to meet you
              As far as Chō-fū-Sa.

                                    By Rihaku (Li T'ai Po)

53

POEM BY THE BRIDGE AT TEN-SHIN

March has come to the bridge head,
Peach boughs and apricot boughs hang over a thousand gates,
At morning there are flowers to cut the heart,
And evening drives them on the eastward-flowing waters.
Petals are on the gone waters and on the going,
        And on the back-swirling eddies,
But to-day's men are not the men of the old days,
Though they hang in the same way over the bridge-rail.

The sea's colour moves at the dawn
And the princes still stand in rows, about the throne,
And the moon falls over the portals of Sei-jō-yō,
And clings to the walls and the gate-top.
With head gear glittering against the cloud and sun,
The lords go forth from the court, and into far borders.
They ride upon dragon-like horses,
Upon horses with head-trappings of yellow metal,
And the streets make way for their passage.
        Haughty their passing,
Haughty their steps as they go in to great banquets,
To high halls and curious food,
To the perfumed air and girls dancing,
To clear flutes and clear singing;
To the dance of the seventy couples;
To the mad chase through the gardens.
Night and day are given over to pleasure
And they think it will last a thousand autumns,
        Unwearying autumns.
For them the yellow dogs howl portents in vain,
And what are they compared to the lady Ryokushu,

That was cause of hate!
Who among them is a man like Han-rei
        Who departed alone with his mistress,
With her hair unbound, and he his own skiffsman!

By Rihaku (Li T'ai Po)

THE JEWEL STAIRS' GRIEVANCE

The jewelled steps are already quite white with dew,
It is so late that the dew soaks my gauze stockings,
And I let down the crystal curtain
And watch the moon through the clear autumn.

By Rihaku (Li T'ai Po)

NOTE: Jewel stairs, therefore a palace. Grievance, therefore there
is something to complain of. Gauze stockings, therefore a court
lady, not a servant who complains. Clear autumn, therefore he has
no excuse on account of weather. Also she has come early, for the
dew has not merely whitened the stairs, but has soaked her stockings.
The poem is especially prized because she utters no direct reproach.

LAMENT OF THE FRONTIER GUARD

By the North Gate, the wind blows full of sand,
Lonely from the beginning of time until now!
Trees fall, the grass goes yellow with autumn.
I climb the towers and towers
        to watch out the barbarous land:
Desolate castle, the sky, the wide desert.
There is no wall left to this village.

Bones white with a thousand frosts,
High heaps, covered with trees and grass;
Who brought this to pass?
Who has brought the flaming imperial anger?
Who has brought the army with drums and with kettle-drums?
Barbarous kings.
A gracious spring, turned to blood-ravenous autumn,
A turmoil of wars-men, spread over the middle kingdom,
Three hundred and sixty thousand,
And sorrow, sorrow like rain.
Sorrow to go, and sorrow, sorrow returning.
Desolate, desolate fields,
And no children of warfare upon them,
        No longer the men for offence and defence.
Ah, how shall you know the dreary sorrow at the North Gate,
With Riboku's name forgotten,
And we guardsmen fed to the tigers.

By Rihaku (Li T'ai Po)

EXILE'S LETTER

Tō So-kiu of Rakuyō, ancient friend, Chancellor Gen.
Now I remember that you built me a special tavern
By the south side of the bridge at Ten-shin.
With yellow gold and white jewels, we paid for songs and
    laughter
And we were drunk for month on month, forgetting the kings
    and princes.
Intelligent men came drifting in from the sea and from the west
    border,

And with them, and with you especially
There was nothing at cross purpose,
And they made nothing of sea-crossing or of mountain-
     crossing,
If only they could be of that fellowship,
And we all spoke out our hearts and minds, and without regret.
And then I was sent off to South Wai,
     smothered in laurel groves,
And you to the north of Raku-hoku,
Till we had nothing but thoughts and memories in common.
And then, when separation had come to its worst,
We met, and travelled into Sen-jō,
Through all the thirty-six folds of the turning and twisting
     waters,
Into a valley of the thousand bright flowers,
That was the first valley;
And into ten thousand valleys full of voices and pine winds.
And with silver harness and reins of gold,
Out came the East of Kan foreman and his company.
And there came also the "True man" of Shi-yō to meet me,
Playing on a jewelled mouth-organ.
In the storied houses of San-ka they gave us more Sennin
     music,
Many instruments, like the sound of young phœnix broods.
The foreman of Kan-chū, drunk, danced
     because his long sleeves wouldn't keep still
With that music playing,
And I, wrapped in brocade, went to sleep with my head on his
     lap,
And my spirit so high it was all over the heavens,
And before the end of the day we were scattered like stars, or
     rain.

I had to be off to So, far away over the waters,
You back to your river-bridge.

And your father, who was brave as a leopard,
Was governor in Hei Shu, and put down the barbarian rabble.
And one May he had you send for me,
        despite the long distance.
And what with broken wheels and so on, I won't say it wasn't
    hard going,
Over roads twisted like sheep's guts.
And I was still going, late in the year,
        in the cutting wind from the North,
And thinking how little you cared for the cost,
        and you caring enough to pay it.
And what a reception:
Red jade cups, food well set on a blue jewelled table,
And I was drunk, and had no thought of returning.
And you would walk out with me to the western corner of the
    castle,
To the dynastic temple, with water about it clear as blue jade,
With boats floating, and the sound of mouth-organs and drums,
With ripples like dragon-scales, going grass green on the water,
Pleasure lasting, with courtezans, going and coming without
    hindrance,
With the willow flakes falling like snow,
And the vermilioned girls getting drunk about sunset,
And the water, a hundred feet deep, reflecting green eyebrows
—Eyebrows painted green are a fine sight in young moonlight,
Gracefully painted—
And the girls singing back at each other,
Dancing in transparent brocade,
And the wind lifting the song, and interrupting it,

Tossing it up under the clouds.
       And all this comes to an end.
       And is not again to be met with.
I went up to the court for examination,
Tried Yō Yū's luck, offered the Chōyō song,
And got no promotion,
       and went back to the East Mountains
       White-headed.
And once again, later, we met at the South bridge-head.
And then the crowd broke up, you went north to San palace,
And if you ask how I regret that parting:
It is like the flowers falling at Spring's end
       Confused, whirled in a tangle.
What is the use of talking, and there is no end of talking,
There is no end of things in the heart.
I call in the boy,
Have him sit on his knees here
       To seal this,
And send it a thousand miles, thinking.

By Rihaku (Li T'ai Po)

TAKING LEAVE OF A FRIEND

Blue mountains to the north of the walls,
White river winding about them;
Here we must make separation
And go out through a thousand miles of dead grass.

Mind like a floating wide cloud,
Sunset like the parting of old acquaintances

Who bow over their clasped hands at a distance.
Our horses neigh to each other
                as we are departing.

                                        By Rihaku (Li T'ai Po)

A BALLAD OF THE MULBERRY ROAD

The sun rises in south east corner of things
To look on the tall house of the Shin
For they have a daughter named Rafu, (pretty girl)
She made the name for herself: "Gauze Veil,"
For she feeds mulberries to silkworms.
She gets them by the south wall of the town.
With green strings she makes the warp of her basket,
She makes the shoulder-straps of her basket
                from the boughs of Katsura,
And she piles her hair up on the left side of her head-piece.

Her earrings are made of pearl,
Her underskirt is of green pattern-silk,
Her overskirt is the same silk dyed in purple,
And when men going by look on Rafu
                They set down their burdens,
They stand and twirl their moustaches.

                        (*Anonymous; Fenollosa Mss., very early; Mori's gloze.*)

60

HUGH SELWYN MAUBERLEY

E. P. ODE POUR L'ELECTION DE SON SEPULCHRE

For three years, out of key with his time,
He strove to resuscitate the dead art
Of poetry; to maintain "the sublime"
In the old sense. Wrong from the start—

No, hardly. but seeing he had been born
In a half savage country, out of date;
Bent resolutely on wringing lilies from the acorn;
Capaneus; trout for factitious bait;

Ἴδμεν γάρ τοι πάνθ', ὅσ' ἐνὶ Τροίη
Caught in the unstopped ear;
Giving the rocks small lee-way
The chopped seas held him, therefore, that year.

His true Penelope was Flaubert,
He fished by obstinate isles;
Observed the elegance of Circe's hair
Rather than the mottoes on sun-dials.

Unaffected by "the march of events,"
He passed from men's memory in *l'an trentuniesme*
De son eage; the case presents
No adjunct to the Muses' diadem.

II

The age demanded an image
Of its accelerated grimace,

Something for the modern stage,
Not, at any rate, an Attic grace;

Not, not certainly, the obscure reveries
Of the inward gaze;
Better mendacities
Than the classics in paraphrase!

The "age demanded" chiefly a mould in plaster,
Made with no loss of time,
A prose kinema, not, not assuredly, alabaster
Or the "sculpture" of rhyme.

III

The tea-rose tea-gown, etc.
Supplants the mousseline of Cos,
The pianola "replaces"
Sappho's barbitos.

Christ follows Dionysus,
Phallic and ambrosial
Made way for macerations;
Caliban casts out Ariel.

All things are a flowing,
Sage Heracleitus says;
But a tawdry cheapness
Shall outlast our days.

Even the Christian beauty
Defects—after Samothrace;

We see τὸ καλόν
Decreed in the market place.

Faun's flesh is not to us,
Nor the saint's vision.
We have the press for wafer;
Franchise for circumcision.

All men, in law, are equals.
Free of Pisistratus,
We choose a knave or an eunuch
To rule over us.

O bright Apollo,
τίν' ἄνδρα, τίν' ἥρωα, τινα θεόν,
What god, man, or hero
Shall I place a tin wreath upon!

IV

These fought in any case,
and some believing,
                    pro domo, in any case . . .

Some quick to arm,
some for adventure,
some from fear of weakness,
some from fear of censure,
some for love of slaughter, in imagination,
learning later . . .
some in fear, learning love of slaughter;

Died some, pro patria,
　　　　　　　non "dulce" non "et decor" . . .
walked eye-deep in hell
believing in old men's lies, then unbelieving
came home, home to a lie,
home to many deceits,
home to old lies and new infamy;
usury age-old and age-thick
and liars in public places.

Daring as never before, wastage as never before.
Young blood and high blood,
fair cheeks, and fine bodies;

fortitude as never before

frankness as never before,
disillusions as never told in the old days,
hysterias, trench confessions,
laughter out of dead bellies.

V

There died a myriad,
And of the best, among them,
For an old bitch gone in the teeth,
For a botched civilization,

Charm, smiling at the good mouth,
Quick eyes gone under earth's lid,

For two gross of broken statues,
For a few thousand battered books.

YEUX GLAUQUES

Gladstone was still respected,
When John Ruskin produced
"Kings' Treasuries"; Swinburne
And Rossetti still abused.

Fœtid Buchanan lifted up his voice
When that faun's head of hers
Became a pastime for
Painters and adulterers.

The Burne-Jones cartons
Have preserved her eyes;
Still, at the Tate, they teach
Cophetua to rhapsodize;

Thin like brook-water,
With a vacant gaze.
The English Rubaiyat was still-born
In those days.

The thin, clear gaze, the same
Still darts out faunlike from the half-ruin'd face,
Questing and passive. . . .
"Ah, poor Jenny's case" . . .

Bewildered that a world
Shows no surprise
At her last maquero's
Adulteries.

"SIENA MI FE'; DISFECEMI MAREMMA"

Among the pickled fœtuses and bottled bones,
Engaged in perfecting the catalogue,
I found the last scion of the
Senatorial families of Strasbourg, Monsieur Verog.

For two hours he talked of Galliffet;
Of Dowson; of the Rhymers' Club;
Told me how Johnson (Lionel) died
By falling from a high stool in a pub . . .

But showed no trace of alcohol
At the autopsy, privately performed—
Tissue preserved—the pure mind
Arose toward Newman as the whiskey warmed.

Dowson found harlots cheaper than hotels;
Headlam for uplift; Image impartially imbued
With raptures for Bacchus, Terpsichore and the Church.
So spoke the author of "The Dorian Mood,"

M. Verog, out of step with the decade,
Detached from his contemporaries,
Neglected by the young,
Because of these reveries.

BRENNBAUM

The skylike limpid eyes,
The circular infant's face,

66

The stiffness from spats to collar
Never relaxing into grace;

The heavy memories of Horeb, Sinai and the forty years,
Showed only when the daylight fell
Level across the face
Of Brennbaum "The Impeccable."

MR. NIXON

In the cream gilded cabin of his steam yacht
Mr. Nixon advised me kindly, to advance with fewer
Dangers of delay. "Consider
        "Carefully the reviewer.

"I was as poor as you are;
"When I began I got, of course,
"Advance on royalties, fifty at first," said Mr. Nixon,
"Follow me, and take a column,
"Even if you have to work free.

"Butter reviewers. From fifty to three hundred
"I rose in eighteen months;
"The hardest nut I had to crack
"Was Dr. Dundas.

"I never mentioned a man but with the view
"Of selling my own works.
"The tip's a good one, as for literature
"It gives no man a sinecure.

"And no one knows, at sight, a masterpiece.
"And give up verse, my boy,
"There's nothing in it."

* * * *

Likewise a friend of Blougram's once advised me:
Don't kick against the pricks,
Accept opinion. The "Nineties" tried your game
And died, there's nothing in it.

X

Beneath the sagging roof
The stylist has taken shelter,
Unpaid, uncelebrated,
At last from the world's welter

Nature receives him;
With a placid and uneducated mistress
He exercises his talents
And the soil meets his distress.

The haven from sophistications and contentions
Leaks through its thatch;
He offers succulent cooking;
The door has a creaking latch.

XI

"Conservatrix of Milésien"
Habits of mind and feeling,
Possibly. But in Ealing
With the most bank-clerkly of Englishmen?

No, "Milesian" is an exaggeration.
No instinct has survived in her
Older than those her grandmother
Told her would fit her station.

XII

"Daphne with her thighs in bark
"Stretches toward me her leafy hands,"—
Subjectively. In the stuffed-satin drawing-room
I await The Lady Valentine's commands,

Knowing my coat has never been
Of precisely the fashion
To stimulate, in her,
A durable passion;

Doubtful, somewhat, of the value
Of well-gowned approbation
Of literary effort,
But never of The Lady Valentine's vocation:

Poetry, her border of ideas,
The edge, uncertain, but a means of blending
With other strata
Where the lower and higher have ending;

A hook to catch the Lady Jane's attention,
A modulation toward the theatre,
Also, in the case of revolution,
A possible friend and comforter.

* * * *

Conduct, on the other hand, the soul
"Which the highest cultures have nourished"
To Fleet St. where
Dr. Johnson flourished;

Beside this thoroughfare
The sale of half-hose has
Long since superseded the cultivation
Of Pierian roses.

ENVOI (1919)

Go, dumb-born book,
Tell her that sang me once that song of Lawes:
Hadst thou but song
As thou hast subjects known,
Then were there cause in thee that should condone
Even my faults that heavy upon me lie,
And build her glories their longevity.

Tell her that sheds
Such treasure in the air,
Recking naught else but that her graces give
Life to the moment,
I would bid them live
As roses might, in magic amber laid,
Red overwrought with orange and all made
One substance and one colour
Braving time.

Tell her that goes
With song upon her lips
But sings not out the song, nor knows
The maker of it, some other mouth,
May be as fair as hers,
Might, in new ages, gain her worshippers,
When our two dusts with Waller's shall be laid,
Siftings on siftings in oblivion,
Till change hath broken down
All things save Beauty alone.

MAUBERLEY (1920)

"Vacuos exercet in aera morsus."

Turned from the "eau-forte
Par Jacquemart"
To the strait head
Of Messalina:

"His true Penelope
Was Flaubert,"
And his tool
The engraver's.

Firmness,
Not the full smile,
His art, but an art
In profile;

Colourless
Pier Francesca,

Pisanello lacking the skill
To forge Achaia.

II

"Qu'est ce qu'ils savent de l'amour, et qu'est ce qu'ils peuvent comprendre?
S'ils ne comprennent pas la poésie, s'ils ne sentent pas la musique, qu'est ce qu'ils peuvent comprendre de cette passion en comparaison avec laquelle la rose est grossière et le parfum des violettes un tonnerre?" CAID ALI

For three years, diabolus in the scale,
He drank ambrosia,
All passes, ANANGKE prevails,
Came end, at last, to that Arcadia.

He had moved amid her phantasmagoria,
Amid her galaxies,
NUKTIS 'AGALMA

    *   *   *   *

Drifted . . . drifted precipitate,
Asking time to be rid of . . .
Of his bewilderment; to designate
His new found orchid. . . .

To be certain . . . certain . . .
(Amid ærial flowers) . . . time for arrangements—
Drifted on
To the final estrangement;

Unable in the supervening blankness
To sift TO AGATHON from the chaff

Until he found his sieve . . .
Ultimately, his seismograph:

—Given that is his "fundamental passion,"
This urge to convey the relation
Of eye-lid and cheek-bone
By verbal manifestation;

To present the series
Of curious heads in medallion—

He had passed, inconscient, full gaze,
The wide-banded irides
And botticellian sprays implied
In their diastasis;

Which anæsthesis, noted a year late,
And weighed, revealed his great affect,
(Orchid), mandate
Of Eros, a retrospect.

   *   *   *   *

Mouths biting empty air,
The still stone dogs,
Caught in metamorphosis, were
Left him as epilogues.

"THE AGE DEMANDED"

Vide Poem II, Page 61

For this agility chance found
Him of all men, unfit

As the red-beaked steeds of
The Cytheræan for a chain bit.

The glow of porcelain
Brought no reforming sense
To his perception
Of the social inconsequence.

Thus, if her colour
Came against his gaze,
Tempered as if
It were through a perfect glaze

He made no immediate application
Of this to relation of the state
To the individual, the month was more temperate
Because this beauty had been.

        The coral isle, the lion-coloured sand
        Burst in upon the porcelain revery:
        Impetuous troubling
        Of his imagery.

Mildness, amid the neo-Nietzschean clatter,
His sense of graduations,
Quite out of place amid
Resistance to current exacerbations,

Invitation, mere invitation to perceptivity
Gradually led him to the isolation
Which these presents place
Under a more tolerant, perhaps, examination.

By constant elimination
The manifest universe
Yielded an armour
Against utter consternation,

A Minoan undulation,
Seen, we admit, amid ambrosial circumstances
Strengthened him against
The discouraging doctrine of chances,

And his desire for survival,
Faint in the most strenuous moods,
Became an Olympian *apathein*
In the presence of selected perceptions.

A pale gold, in the aforesaid pattern,
The unexpected palms
Destroying, certainly, the artist's urge,
Left him delighted with the imaginary
Audition of the phantasmal sea-surge,

Incapable of the least utterance or composition,
Emendation, conservation of the "better tradition,"
Refinement of medium, elimination of superfluities,
August attraction or concentration.

Nothing, in brief, but maudlin confession,
Irresponse to human aggression,
Amid the precipitation, down-float
Of insubstantial manna,
Lifting the faint susurrus
Of his subjective hosannah.

Ultimate affronts to
Human redundancies;

Non-esteem of self-styled "his betters"
Leading, as he well knew,
To his final
Exclusion from the world of letters.

IV

Scattered Moluccas
Not knowing, day to day,
The first day's end, in the next noon;
The placid water
Unbroken by the Simoon;

Thick foliage
Placid beneath warm suns,
Tawn fore-shores
Washed in the cobalt of oblivions;

Or through dawn-mist
The grey and rose
Of the juridical
Flamingoes;

A consciousness disjunct,
Being but this overblotted
Series
Of intermittences;

Coracle of Pacific voyages,
The unforecasted beach;
Then on an oar
Read this:

"I was
"And I no more exist;
"Here drifted
"An hedonist."

MEDALLION

Luini in porcelain!
The grand piano
Utters a profane
Protest with her clear soprano.

The sleek head emerges
From the gold-yellow frock
As Anadyomene in the opening
Pages of Reinach.

Honey-red, closing the face-oval,
A basket-work of braids which seem as if they were
Spun in King Minos' hall
From metal, or intractable amber;

The face-oval beneath the glaze,
Bright in its suave bounding-line, as,
Beneath half-watt rays,
The eyes turn topaz.

from HOMAGE TO SEX-
TUS PROPERTIUS

I

Shades of Callimachus, Coan ghosts of Philetas
It is in your grove I would walk,
I who come first from the clear font
Bringing the Grecian orgies into Italy,
                  and the dance into Italy.
Who hath taught you so subtle a measure,
             in what hall have you heard it;
What foot beat out your time-bar,
          what water has mellowed your whistles?

Out-weariers of Apollo will, as we know, continue their Mar-
   tian generalities,
      We have kept our erasers in order.
A new-fangled chariot follows the flower-hung horses;
A young Muse with young loves clustered about her
          ascends with me into the æther, . . .
And there is no high-road to the Muses.

Annalists will continue to record Roman reputations,
Celebrities from the Trans-Caucasus will belaud Roman celeb-
   rities
And expound the distentions of Empire,
But for something to read in normal circumstances?
For a few pages brought down from the forked hill unsullied?
I ask a wreath which will not crush my head.
         And there is no hurry about it;
I shall have, doubtless, a boom after my funeral,

Seeing that long standing increases all things
                                    regardless of quality.

And who would have known the towers
                        pulled down by a deal-wood horse;
Or of Achilles withstaying waters by Simois
Or of Hector spattering wheel-rims,
Or of Polydmantus, by Scamander, or Helenus and Deiphoi-
    bos?
Their door-yards would scarcely know them, or Paris.
Small talk O Ilion, and O Troad
                            twice taken by Oetian gods,
If Homer had not stated your case!

And I also among the later nephews of this city
                        shall have my dog's day,
With no stone upon my contemptible sepulchre;
My vote coming from the temple of Phoebus in Lycia, at
    Patara,
And in the meantime my songs will travel,
And the devirginated young ladies will enjoy them
                when they have got over the strangeness,
For Orpheus tamed the wild beasts—
                        and held up the Threician river;
And Citharaon shook up the rocks by Thebes
            and danced them into a bulwark at his pleasure,
And you, O Polyphemus? Did harsh Galatea almost
Turn to your dripping horses, because of a tune, under Aetna?
We must look into the matter.
Bacchus and Apollo in favour of it,
There will be a crowd of young women doing homage to my
    palaver,

Though my house is not propped up by Taenarian columns
    from Laconia (associated with Neptune and Cerberus),
Though it is not stretched upon gilded beams;
My orchards do not lie level and wide
                        as the forests of Phaecia,
                    the luxurious and Ionian,
Nor are my caverns stuffed stiff with a Marcian vintage,
My cellar does not date from Numa Pompilius,
Nor bristle with wine jars,
Nor is it equipped with a frigidaire patent;
Yet the companions of the Muses
            will keep their collective nose in my books,
And weary with historical data, they will turn to my dance
    tune.

Happy who are mentioned in my pamphlets,
        the songs shall be a fine tomb-stone over their beauty.
                But against this?
Neither expensive pyramids scraping the stars in their route,
Nor houses modelled upon that of Jove in East Elis,
Nor the monumental effigies of Mausolus,
                are a complete elucidation of death.

Flame burns, rain sinks into the cracks
And they all go to rack ruin beneath the thud of the years
Stands genius a deathless adornment,
        a name not to be worn out with the years.

III

Midnight, and a letter comes to me from
            our mistress:

Telling me to come to Tibur:
                    At once!!
"Bright tips reach up from twin towers,
"Anienan spring water falls into flat-spread pools."

What *is* to be done about it?
        Shall I entrust myself to entangled shadows,
Where bold hands may do violence to my person?

Yet if I postpone my obedience
                    because of this respectable terror,
I shall be prey to lamentations worse than a nocturnal assailant.
And I shall be in the wrong,
                    and it will last a twelve-month,
For her hands have no kindness me-ward,
Nor is there anyone to whom lovers are not sacred
    at midnight
        And in the Via Sciro.
If any man would be a lover
                he may walk on the Scythian coast,
No barbarism would go to the extent of doing him harm,
The moon will carry his candle,
                the stars will point out the stumbles,
Cupid will carry lighted torches before him
                and keep mad dogs off his ankles.
Thus all roads are perfectly safe
                    and at any hour;
Who so indecorous as to shed the pure gore of a suitor?!
        Cypris is his cicerone.

What if undertakers follow my track,
                such a death is worth dying.

81

She would bring frankincense and wreaths to my tomb,
    She would sit like an ornament on my pyre.

Gods' aid, let not my bones lie in a public location
With crowds too assiduous in their crossing of it;
For thus are tombs of lovers most desecrated.

May a woody and sequestered place cover me with its foliage
Or may I inter beneath the hummock
                of some as yet uncatalogued sand;
At any rate I shall not have my epitaph in a high road.

IV

DIFFERENCE OF OPINION WITH LYGDAMUS

Tell me the truths which you hear of our constant young lady,
                Lygdamus,
And may the bought yoke of a mistress lie with
                equitable weight on your shoulders;
For I am swelled up with inane pleasurabilities
                and deceived by your reference
To things which you think I would like to believe.

No messenger should come wholly empty,
                and a slave should fear plausibilities;
Much conversation is as good as having a home.
    Out with it, tell it to me, all of it, from the beginning
I guzzle with outstretched ears.
Thus? She wept into uncombed hair,
                                And you saw it.

Vast waters flowed from her eyes?

                     You, you Lygdamus

Saw her stretched on her bed,—

                  it was no glimpse in a mirror;

No gawds on her snowy hands, no orfevrerie,

Sad garment draped on her slender arms.

Her escritoires lay shut by the bed-feet.

Sadness hung over the house, and the desolated female attendants

Were desolated because she had told them her dreams.

She was veiled in the midst of that place,

Damp woolly handkerchiefs were stuffed into her
        undryable eyes,

And a querulous noise responded to our solicitous reprobations.

For which things you will get a reward from me, Lygdamus?

To say many things is equal to having a home.

And the other woman "has not enticed me

                  by her pretty manners,

"She has caught me with herbaceous poison,

        she twiddles the spiked wheel of a rhombus,

"She stews puffed frogs, snake's bones, the moulted feathers of
        screech owls,

"She binds me with ravvles of shrouds.

        "Black spiders spin in her bed!

"Let her lovers snore at her in the morning!

        "May the gout cramp up her feet!

"Does he like me to sleep here alone,

        Lygdamus?

Will he say nasty things at my funeral?"

And you expect me to believe this

        after twelve months of discomfort?

V

Now if ever it is time to cleanse Helicon;

        to lead Emathian horses afield,

And to name over the census of my chiefs in the Roman camp.

If I have not the faculty, "The bare attempt would be praise-
worthy."

"In things of similar magnitude

               the mere will to act is sufficient."

The primitive ages sang Venus,

             the last sings of a tumult,

And I also will sing war when this matter of a girl is exhausted.

I with my beak hauled ashore would proceed in a more stately
manner,

My Muse is eager to instruct me in a new gamut, or gambetto,

Up, up my soul, from your lowly cantilation,

               put on a timely vigour.

Oh august Pierides! Now for a large-mouthed product.

Thus:

"The Euphrates denies its protection to the Parthian and
apologizes for Crassus,"

And "It is, I think, India which now gives necks to your
triumph,"

And so forth, Augustus. "Virgin Arabia shakes in her inmost
dwelling."

If any land shrink into a distant seacoast,

        it is a mere postponement of your domination.

And I shall follow the camp, I shall be duly celebrated for
singing the affairs of your cavalry.

May the fates watch over my day.

Yet you ask on what account I write so many love-lyrics
And whence this soft book comes into my mouth.
Neither Calliope nor Apollo sung these things into my ear,
    My genius is no more than a girl.

If she with ivory fingers drive a tune through the lyre,
    We look at the process.
How easy the moving fingers; if hair is mussed on her forehead,
If she goes in a gleam of Cos, in a slither of dyed stuff,
There is a volume in the matter; if her eyelids sink into sleep,
There are new jobs for the author;
And if she plays with me with her shirt off,
    We shall construct many Iliads.
And whatever she does or says
    We shall spin long yarns out of nothing.
Thus much the fates have allotted me, and if, Maecenas,
I were able to lead heroes into armour, I would not,
Neither would I warble of Titans, nor of Ossa
                    spiked onto Olympus,
Nor of causeways over Pelion,
Nor of Thebes in its ancient respectability,
            nor of Homer's reputation in Pergamus,
Nor of Xerxes' two-barreled kingdom, nor of
    Remus and his royal family,
Nor of dignified Carthaginian characters,
Nor of Welsh mines and the profit Marus had out of them.

I should remember Caesar's affairs . . .
                   for a background,
Although Callimachus did without them,

and without Theseus,
Without an inferno, without Achilles attended of gods,
Without Ixion, and without the sons of Menoetius and the
Argo and without Jove's grave and the Titans.

And my ventricles do not palpitate to Caesarial *ore ro-
tundos*,
Nor to the tune of the Phrygian fathers.
Sailor, of winds; a plowman, concerning his oxen;
Soldier, the enumeration of wounds; the sheep-feeder, of ewes;
We, in our narrow bed, turning aside from battles:
Each man where he can, wearing out the day in his manner.

It is noble to die of love, and honourable to remain
uncuckolded for a season.
And she speaks ill of light women,
and will not praise Homer
Because Helen's conduct is "unsuitable."

VI

When, when, and whenever death closes our eyelids,
Moving naked over Acheron
Upon the one raft, victor and conquered together,
Marius and Jugurtha together,
one tangle of shadows.

Caesar plots against India,
Tigris and Euphrates shall, from now on, flow at his bidding,
Tibet shall be full of Roman policemen,
The Parthians shall get used to our statuary
and acquire a Roman religion;

One raft on the veiled flood of Acheron,
      Marius and Jugurtha together.

Nor at my funeral either will there be any long trail,
             bearing ancestral lares and images;
No trumpets filled with my emptiness,
Nor shall it be on an Atalic bed;
      The perfumed cloths will be absent.
A small plebeian procession.
      Enough, enough and in plenty
There will be three books at my obsequies
Which I take, my not unworthy gift, to Persephone.

You will follow the bare scarified breast
Nor will you be weary of calling my name, nor too weary
      To place the last kiss on my lips
When the Syrian onyx is broken.

        "He who is now vacant dust
        "Was once the slave of one passion:"
Give that much inscription
        "Death why tardily come?"

You, sometimes, will lament a lost friend,
      For it is a custom:
This care for past men,

Since Adonis was gored in Idalia, and the Cytharean
Ran crying with out-spread hair,
      In vain, you call back the shade,
In vain, Cynthia. Vain call to unanswering shadow,
      Small talk comes from small bones.

VII

Me happy, night, night full of brightness;
Oh couch made happy by my long delectations;
How many words talked out with abundant candles;
Struggles when the lights were taken away;
Now with bared breasts she wrestled against me,
                Tunic spread in delay;
And she then opening my eyelids fallen in sleep,
Her lips upon them; and it was her mouth saying:
    Sluggard!

In how many varied embraces, our changing arms,
Her kisses, how many, lingering on my lips.
"Turn not Venus into a blinded motion,
            Eyes are the guides of love,
Paris took Helen naked coming from the bed of Menelaus,
Endymion's naked body, bright bait for Diana,"
          —such at least is the story.

While our fates twine together, sate we our eyes with love;
For long night comes upon you
              and a day when no day returns.
Let the gods lay chains upon us
              so that no day shall unbind them.

Fool who would set a term to love's madness,
For the sun shall drive with black horses,
           earth shall bring wheat from barley,
The flood shall move toward the fountain
           Ere love know moderations,
           The fish shall swim in dry streams.
No, now while it may be, let not the fruit of life cease.

Dry wreaths drop their petals,
        their stalks are woven in baskets,
To-day we take the great breath of lovers,
        to-morrow fate shuts us in.

Though you give all your kisses
                you give but few.

Nor can I shift my pains to other,
        Hers will I be dead,
If she confer such nights upon me,
                long is my life, long in years,
If she give me many,
        God am I for the time.

IX

1

The twisted rhombs ceased their clamour of accompaniment;
The scorched laurel lay in the fire-dust;
The moon still declined to descend out of heaven,

But the black ominous owl hoot was audible.

And one raft bears our fates
                on the veiled lake toward Avernus
Sails spread on Cerulean waters, I would shed tears
        for two;
I shall live, if she continue in life,
        If she dies, I shall go with her.

Great Zeus, save the woman,
                or she will sit before your feet in a veil,
                and tell out the long list of her troubles.

2

Persephone and Dis, Dis, have mercy upon her,
There are enough women in hell,
                        quite enough beautiful women,
Iope, and Tyro, and Pasiphae, and the formal girls of Achaia,
And out of Troad, and from the Campania,
Death has his tooth in the lot,
                        Avernus lusts for the lot of them,
Beauty is not eternal, no man has perennial fortune,
Slow foot, or swift foot, death delays but for a season.

3

My light, light of my eyes,
                you are escaped from great peril,
Go back to Great Dian's dances bearing suitable gifts,
Pay up your vow of night watches
                        to Dian, goddess of virgins,
And unto me also pay debt:
The ten nights of your company you have
                        promised me.

X

Light, light of my eyes, at an exceeding late
        hour I was wandering,
And intoxicated,
                and no servant was leading me,

And a minute crowd of small boys came from opposite,
             I do not know what boys,
And I am afraid of numerical estimate,
And some of them shook little torches,
             and others held onto arrows,
And the rest laid their chains upon me,
          and they were naked, the lot of them,
And one of the lot was given to lust.

"That incensed female has consigned him to our pleasure."
So spoke. And the noose was over my neck.
And another said "Get him plumb in the middle!
       "Shove along there, shove along!"
And another broke in upon this:
            "He thinks that we are not gods."
"And she has been waiting for the scoundrel,
          and in a new Sidonian night cap,
And with more than Arabian odours,
          God knows where he has been.
She could scarcely keep her eyes open
           enter that much for his bail.
               Get along now!"

We were coming near to the house,
          and they gave another yank to my cloak,
And it was morning, and I wanted to see if she was
    alone, and resting,
And Cynthia was alone in her bed.
               I was stupefied.
I had never seen her looking so beautiful.
    No, not when she was tunick'd in purple.

Such aspect was presented to me, me recently
        emerged from my visions,
You will observe that pure form has its value.

"You are a very early inspector of mistresses.
"Do you think I have adopted your habits?"
                There were upon the bed no signs of a
                        voluptuous encounter,
                No signs of a second incumbent.

She continued:
                "No incubus has crushed his body against me,
                "Though spirits are celebrated for adultery.
                "And I am going to the temple of Vesta . . ."
                        and so on.

Since that day I have had no pleasant nights.

XII

Who, who will be the next man to entrust his girl to a friend?
Love interferes with fidelities;
The gods have brought shame on their relatives;
Each man wants the pomegranate for himself;
Amiable and harmonious people are pushed incontinent into
        duels,
A Trojan and adulterous person came to Menelaus under the
        rites of hospitium,
And there was a case in Colchis, Jason and that woman in
        Colchis;
And besides, Lynceus,
                you were drunk.

Could you endure such promiscuity?
                    She was not renowned for fidelity;
But to jab a knife in my vitals, to have passed on a swig of
        poison,
Preferable, my dear boy, my dear Lynceus,
Comrade, comrade of my life, of my purse, of my person;
But in one bed, in one bed alone, my dear Lynceus
                    I deprecate your attendance;
I would ask a like boon of Jove.

And you write of Achelöus, who contended with Hercules,
You write of Adrastus' horses and the funeral rites of Achenor,
And you will not leave off imitating Aeschylus.
                    Though you make a hash of Antimachus,
You think you are going to do Homer.
                    And still a girl scorns the gods,
Of all these young women
            not one has enquired the cause of the world,
Nor the modus of lunar eclipses
            Nor whether there be any patch left of us
After we cross the infernal ripples,
            nor if the thunder fall from predestination;
Nor anything else of importance.

Upon the Actian marshes Virgil is Phoebus' chief of police,
            He can tabulate Caesar's great ships.
He thrills to Ilian arms,
            He shakes the Trojan weapons of Aeneas,
And casts stores on Lavinian beaches.

Make way, ye Roman authors,
                    clear the street, O ye Greeks,

For a much larger Iliad is in the course of construction
(and to Imperial order)
Clear the streets, O ye Greeks!

And you also follow him "neath Phrygian pine shade:
      Thyrsis and Daphnis upon whittled reeds,
And how ten sins can corrupt young maidens;
      Kids for a bribe and pressed udders,
Happy selling poor loves for cheap apples.

Tityrus might have sung the same vixen;
      Corydon tempted Alexis,
Head farmers do likewise, and lying weary amid their oats
They get praise from tolerant Hamadryads."
Go on, to Ascraeus' prescription, the ancient,
          respected, Wordsworthian:
"A flat field for rushes, grapes grow on the slope."

And behold me, small fortune left in my house.
Me, who had no general for a grandfather!
I shall triumph among young ladies of indeterminate character,
My talent acclaimed in their banquets,
      I shall be honoured with yesterday's
        wreaths.
And the god strikes to the marrow.

      Like a trained and performing tortoise,
I would make verse in your fashion, if she should
    command it,
With her husband asking a remission of sentence,
      And even this infamy would not attract
        numerous readers

Were there an erudite or violent passion,
For the nobleness of the populace brooks nothing below its
    own altitude.
One must have resonance, resonance and sonority
        . . . like a goose.

Varro sang Jason's expedition,
            Varro, of his great passion Leucadia,
There is song in the parchment; Catullus the highly
            indecorous,
Of Lesbia, known above Helen;
And in the dyed pages of Calvus,
            Calvus mourning Quintilia,
And but now Gallus had sung of Lycoris.
        Fair, fairest Lycoris—
The waters of Styx poured over the wound:
And now Propertius of Cynthia, taking his stand among these.

CANTOS

CANTO I

And then went down to the ship,
Set keel to breakers, forth on the godly sea, and
We set up mast and sail on that swart ship,
Bore sheep aboard her, and our bodies also
Heavy with weeping, and winds from sternward
Bore us out onward with bellying canvas,
Circe's this craft, the trim-coifed goddess.
Then sat we amidships, wind jamming the tiller,
Thus with stretched sail, we went over sea till day's end.
Sun to his slumber, shadows o'er all the ocean,
Came we then to the bounds of deepest water,
To the Kimmerian lands, and peopled cities
Covered with close-webbed mist, unpierced ever
With glitter of sun-rays
Nor with stars stretched, nor looking back from heaven
Swartest night stretched over wretched men there.
The ocean flowing backward, came we then to the place
Aforesaid by Circe.
Here did they rites, Perimedes and Eurylochus,
And drawing sword from my hip
I dug the ell-square pitkin;
Poured we libations unto each the dead,
First mead and then sweet wine, water mixed with white flour
Then prayed I many a prayer to the sickly death's-heads;
As set in Ithaca, sterile bulls of the best
For sacrifice, heaping the pyre with goods,
A sheep to Tiresias only, black and a bell-sheep.
Dark blood flowed in the fosse,

Souls out of Erebus, cadaverous dead, of brides
Of youths and of the old who had borne much;
Souls stained with recent tears, girls tender,
Men many, mauled with bronze lance heads,
Battle spoil, bearing yet dreory arms,
These many crowded about me; with shouting,
Pallor upon me, cried to my men for more beasts;
Slaughtered the herds, sheep slain of bronze;
Poured ointment, cried to the gods,
To Pluto the strong, and praised Proserpine;
Unsheathed the narrow sword,
I sat to keep off the impetuous impotent dead,
Till I should hear Tiresias.
But first Elpenor came, our friend Elpenor,
Unburied, cast on the wide earth,
Limbs that we left in the house of Circe,
Unwept, unwrapped in sepulchre, since toils urged other.
Pitiful spirit. And I cried in hurried speech:
"Elpenor, how art thou come to this dark coast?
"Cam'st thou afoot, outstripping seamen?"
          And he in heavy speech:
"Ill fate and abundant wine. I slept in Circe's ingle.
"Going down the long ladder unguarded,
"I fell against the buttress,
"Shattered the nape-nerve, the soul sought Avernus.
"But thou, O King, I bid remember me, unwept, unburied,
"Heap up mine arms, be tomb by sea-bord, and inscribed:
"*A man of no fortune, and with a name to come.*
"And set my oar up, that I swung mid fellows."

And Anticlea came, whom I beat off, and then Tiresias Theban,
Holding his golden wand, knew me, and spoke first:

"A second time? why? man of ill star,
"Facing the sunless dead and this joyless region?
"Stand from the fosse, leave me my bloody bever
"For soothsay."
                    And I stepped back,
And he strong with the blood, said then: "Odysseus
"Shalt return through spiteful Neptune, over dark seas,
"Lose all companions." Then Anticlea came.
Lie quiet Divus. I mean, that is Andreas Divus,
In officina Wecheli, 1538, out of Homer.
And he sailed, by Sirens and thence outward and away
And unto Circe.
                    Venerandam,
In the Cretan's phrase, with the golden crown, Aphrodite,
Cypri munimenta sortita est, mirthful, oricalchi, with golden
Girdle and breast bands, thou with dark eyelids
Bearing the golden bough of Argicida. So that:

CANTO II

Hang it all, Robert Browning,
there can be but the one "Sordello."
But Sordello, and my Sordello?
Lo Sordels si fo di Mantovana.
So-shu churned in the sea.
Seal sports in the spray-whited circles of cliff-wash,
Sleek head, daughter of Lir,
                    eyes of Picasso
Under black fur-hood, lithe daughter of Ocean;
And the wave runs in the beach-groove:
"Eleanor, ἐλέναυς and ἐλέπτολις!"
                    And poor old Homer blind, blind, as a bat,

Ear, ear for the sea-surge, murmur of old men's voices:
"Let her go back to the ships,
"Back among Grecian faces, lest evil come on our own,
"Evil and further evil, and a curse cursed on our children,
"Moves, yes she moves like a goddess
"And has the face of a god
                    and the voice of Schoeney's daughters,
"And doom goes with her in walking,
"Let her go back to the ships,
                    back among Grecian voices."
And by the beach-run, Tyro,
                    Twisted arms of the sea-god,
Lithe sinews of water, gripping her, cross-hold,
And the blue-gray glass of the wave tents them,
Glare azure of water, cold-welter, close cover.
Quiet sun-tawny sand-stretch,
The gulls broad out their wings,
                    nipping between the splay feathers;
Snipe come for their bath,
                    bend out their wing-joints,
Spread wet wings to the sun-film,
And by Scios,
                    to left of the Naxos passage,
Naviform rock overgrown,
                    algæ cling to its edge,
There is a wine-red glow in the shallows,
                    a tin flash in the sun-dazzle.

The ship landed in Scios,
                    men wanting spring-water,
And by the rock-pool a young boy loggy with vine-must,
                    "To Naxos? Yes, we'll take you to Naxos,

99

Cum' along lad." "Not that way!"
"Aye, that way is Naxos."
        And I said: "It's a straight ship."
And an ex-convict out of Italy
        knocked me into the fore-stays,
(He was wanted for manslaughter in Tuscany)
        And the whole twenty against me,
Mad for a little slave money.
        And they took her out of Scios
And off her course...
        And the boy came to, again, with the racket,
And looked out over the bows,
        and to eastward, and to the Naxos passage.
God-sleight then, god-sleight:
        Ship stock fast in sea-swirl,
Ivy upon the oars, King Pentheus,
        grapes with no seed but sea-foam,
Ivy in scupper-hole.
Aye, I, Acœtes, stood there,
        and the god stood by me,
Water cutting under the keel,
Sea-break from stern forrards,
        wake running off from the bow,
And where was gunwhale, there now was vine-trunk,
And tenthril where cordage had been,
        grape-leaves on the rowlocks,
Heavy vine on the oarshafts,
And, out of nothing, a breathing,
        hot breath on my ankles,
Beasts like shadows in glass,
        a furred tail upon nothingness.
Lynx-purr, and heathery smell of beasts,

where tar smell had been,
Sniff and pad-foot of beasts,
                    eye-glitter out of black air.
The sky overshot, dry, with no tempest,
Sniff and pad-foot of beasts,
                    fur brushing my knee-skin,
Rustle of airy sheaths,
                    dry forms in the *æther*.
And the ship like a keel in ship-yard,
                    slung like an ox in smith's sling,
Ribs stuck fast in the ways,
                    grape-cluster over pin-rack,
                    void air taking pelt.
Lifeless air become sinewed,
                    feline leisure of panthers,
Leopards sniffing the grape shoots by scupper-hole,
Crouched panthers by fore-hatch,
And the sea blue-deep about us,
                    green-ruddy in shadows,
And Lyæus: "From now, Accœtes, my altars,
Fearing no bondage,
                    fearing no cat of the wood,
Safe with my lynxes,
                    feeding grapes to my leopards,
Olibanum is my incense,
                    the vines grow in my homage."

The back-swell now smooth in the rudder-chains,
Black snout of a porpoise
                    where Lycabs had been,
Fish-scales on the oarsmen.
          And I worship.

I have seen what I have seen.

       When they brought the boy I said:
"He has a god in him,
         though I do not know which god."
And they kicked me into the fore-stays.
I have seen what I have seen:
       Medon's face like the face of a dory,
Arms shrunk into fins. And you, Pentheus,
Had as well listen to Tiresias, and to Cadmus,
       or your luck will go out of you.
Fish-scales over groin muscles,
       lynx-purr amid sea...
And of a later year,
       pale in the wine-red algæ,
If you will lean over the rock,
       the coral face under wave-tinge,
Rose-paleness under water-shift,
       Ileuthyeria, fair Dafne of sea-bords,
The swimmer's arms turned to branches,
Who will say in what year,
       fleeing what band of tritons,
The smooth brows, seen, and half seen,
       now ivory stillness.

And So-shu churned in the sea, So-shu also,
       using the long moon for a churn-stick...
Lithe turning of water,
       sinews of Poseidon,
Black azure and hyaline,
       glass wave over Tyro,
Close cover, unstillness,
       bright welter of wave-cords,

Then quiet water,
        quiet in the buff sands,
Sea-fowl stretching wing-joints,
        splashing in rock-hollows and sand-hollows
In the wave-runs by the half-dune;
Glass-glint of wave in the tide-rips against sunlight,
        pallor of Hesperus,
Grey peak of the wave,
        wave, colour of grape's pulp,

Olive grey in the near,
        far, smoke grey of the rock-slide,
Salmon-pink wings of the fish-hawk
        cast grey shadows in water,
The tower like a one-eyed great goose
        cranes up out of the olive-grove,

And we have heard the fauns chiding Proteus
        in the smell of hay under the olive-trees,
And the frogs singing against the fauns
        in the half-light.
And...

CANTO III

I sat on the Dogana's steps
For the gondolas cost too much, that year,
And there were not "those girls," there was one face,
And the Buccentoro twenty yards off, howling "Stretti,"
The lit cross-beams, that year, in the Morosini,
And peacocks in Koré's house, or there may have been.
        Gods float in the azure air,

Bright gods and Tuscan, back before dew was shed.
Light: and the first light, before ever dew was fallen.
Panisks, and from the oak, dryas,
And from the apple, mælid,
Through all the wood, and the leaves are full of voices,
A-whisper, and the clouds bowe over the lake,
And there are gods upon them,
And in the water, the almond-white swimmers,
The silvery water glazes the upturned nipple,
   As Poggio has remarked.
Green veins in the turquoise,
Or, the gray steps lead up under the cedars.

My Cid rode up to Burgos,
Up to the studded gate between two towers,
Beat with his lance butt, and the child came out,
Una niña de nueve años,
To the little gallery over the gate, between the towers,
Reading the writ, voce tinnula:
That no man speak to, feed, help Ruy Diaz,
On pain to have his heart out, set on a pike spike
And both his eyes torn out, and all his goods sequestered,
"And here, Myo Cid, are the seals,
The big seal and the writing."
And he came down from Bivar, Myo Cid,
With no hawks left there on their perches,
And no clothes there in the presses,
And left his trunk with Raquel and Vidas,
That big box of sand, with the pawn-brokers,
To get pay for his menie;
Breaking his way to Valencia.
Ignez da Castro murdered, and a wall

Here stripped, here made to stand.
Drear waste, the pigment flakes from the stone,
Or plaster flakes, Mantegna painted the wall.
Silk tatters, "Nec Spe Nec Metu."

from CANTO IV

Palace in smoky light,
Troy but a heap of smouldering boundary stones,
ANAXIFORMINGES! Aurunculeia!
Hear me. Cadmus of Golden Prows!
The silver mirrors catch the bright stones and flare,
Dawn, to our waking, drifts in the green cool light;
Dew-haze blurs, in the grass, pale ankles moving.
Beat, beat, whirr, thud, in the soft turf
          under the apple trees,
Choros nympharum, goat-foot, with the pale foot alternate;
Crescent of blue-shot waters, green-gold in the shallows,
A black cock crows in the sea-foam;
And by the curved, carved foot of the couch,
          claw-foot and lion head, an old man seated
Speaking in the low drone . . . :
                    Ityn!
Et ter flebiliter, Ityn, Ityn!
And she went toward the window and cast her down,
          "All the while, the while, swallows crying:
Ityn!
          "It is Cabestan's heart in the dish."
          "It is Cabestan's heart in the dish?
          "No other taste shall change this."
And she went toward the window,
               the slim white stone bar

Making a double arch;
Firm even fingers held to the firm pale stone;
Swung for a moment,
            and the wind out of Rhodez
Caught in the full of her sleeve.
        . . . the swallows crying:
'Tis. 'Tis. Ytis!
. . .

CANTO IX

One year floods rose,
One year they fought in the snows,
One year hail fell, breaking the trees and walls.
Down here in the marsh they trapped him
        in one year,
And he stood in the water up to his neck
        to keep the hounds off him,
And he floundered about in the marsh
        and came in after three days,
That was Astorre Manfredi of Faenza
        who worked the ambush
        and set the dogs off to find him,
In the marsh, down here under Mantua,
And he fought in Fano, in a street fight,
        and that was nearly the end of him;
And the Emperor came down and knighted us,
And they had a wooden castle set up for fiesta,
And one year Basinio went out into the courtyard
        Where the lists were, and the palisades
        had been set for the tourneys,
And he talked down the anti-Hellene,

And there was an heir male to the seignor,
And Madame Genevra died.
And he, Sigismundo, was Capitan for the Venetians.
And he had sold off small castles
            and built the great Rocca to his plan,
And he fought like ten devils at Monteluro
            and got nothing but the victory
And old Sforza bitched us at Pèsaro;
            (*sic*) March the 16th:
"that Messire Alessandro Sforza
            is become lord of Pèsaro
"through the wangle of the Illus. Sgr. Mr. Fedricho d'Orbino
"Who worked the wangle with Galeaz
            "through the wiggling of Messr Francesco,
"Who waggled it so that Galeaz should sell Pèsaro
            "to Alex and Fossembrone to Feddy;
"and he hadn't the right to sell.
"And this he did *bestialmente;* that is Sforza did *bestialmente*
"as he had promised him, Sigismundo, *per capitoli*
            "to see that he, Malatesta, should have Pèsaro."
And this cut us off from our south half
            and finished our game, thus, in the beginning,
And he, Sigismundo, spoke his mind to Francesco
            and we drove them out of the Marches.

And the King o' Ragona, Alphonse le roy d'Aragon,
            was the next nail in our coffin,
And all you can say is, anyway,
that he Sigismundo called a town council
And Valturio said "as well for a sheep as a lamb"
            and this change-over (*hæc traditio*)
As old bladder said "*rem eorum saluavit*"

Saved the Florentine state; and that, maybe, was something.
And "Florence our natural ally" as they said in the meeting
        for whatever that was worth afterward.
And he began building the TEMPIO,
        and Polixena, his second wife, died.
And the Venetians sent down an ambassador
And said "speak humanely,
"But tell him it's no time for raising his pay."
And the Venetians sent down an ambassador
        with three pages of secret instructions
To the effect: Did he think the campaign was a joy-ride?
And old Wattle-wattle slipped into Milan
But he couldn't stand Sidg being so high with the Venetians
And he talked it over with Feddy; and Feddy said "Pèsaro"
And old Foscari wrote "*Caro mio*
"If we split with Francesco you can have it
"And we'll help you in every way possible."
        But Feddy offered it sooner.
And Sigismundo got up a few arches,
And stole that marble in Classe, "stole" that is,
Casus est talis:
        Foscari doge, to the prefect of Ravenna
"Why, what, which, thunder, damnation????"

Casus est talis:
        Filippo, commendatary of the abbazia
Of Sant Apollinaire, Classe, Cardinal of Bologna
That he did one night (*quadam nocte*) sell to the
Illmo D^o, D^o Sigismund Malatesta
Lord of Arimnium, marble, porphyry, serpentine,
Whose men, Sigismundo's, came with more than an hundred
two wheeled ox carts and deported, for the beautifying

of the *tempio* where was Santa Maria in Trivio
Where the same are now on the walls. Four hundred
ducats to be paid back to the *abbazia* by the said swindling
Cardinal or his heirs.
        grnnh! rrnnh, pthg.
wheels, plaustra, oxen under night-shield,
And on the 13th of August: Aloysius Purtheo,
The next abbot, to Sigismundo, receipt for 200 ducats
Corn-salve for the damage done in that scurry.

And there was the row about that German-Burgundian female
And it was his messianic year, Poliorcetes,
        but he was being a bit too POLUMETIS
And the Venetians wouldn't give him six months' vacation.

And he went down to the old brick heap of Pèsaro
        and waited for Feddy
And Feddy finally said "I am coming!...
        ...to help Alessandro."
And he said: "This time Mister Feddy has done it."
He said: "Broglio, I'm the goat. This time
        Mr. Feddy has done it (*m'l'a calata*)."
And he'd lost his job with the Venetians,
And the stone didn't come in from Istria:
And we sent men to the silk war;
And Wattle never paid up on the nail
        Though we signed on with Milan and Florence;
And he set up the bombards in muck down by Vada
        where nobody else could have set 'em
and he took the wood out of the bombs
        and made 'em of two scoops of metal
And the jobs getting smaller and smaller,

Until he signed on with Siena;
And that time they grabbed his post-bag.
And what was it, anyhow?
Pitigliano, a man with a ten acre lot,
Two lumps of tufa,
and they'd taken his pasture land from him,
And Sidg had got back their horses,
and he had two big lumps of tufa
with six hundred pigs in the basements.
And the poor devils were dying of cold.
And this is what they found in the post-bag:
Ex Arimino die xx Decembris
"Magnifice ac potens domine, mi singularissime
"I advise yr. Lordship how
"I have been with master Alwidge who
"has shown me the design of the nave that goes in the middle,
"of the church and the design for the roof and..."
"JHesus,
"Magnifico exso. Signor Mio
"Sence to-day I am recommanded that I have to tel you my
"father's opinium that he has shode to Mr. Genare about the
"valts of the cherch... etc ...

   "Giovane of Master alwise P. S. I think it advisabl that
"I shud go to rome to talk to mister Albert so as I can no
"what he thinks about it rite.

"Sagramoro..."

"Illustre signor mio, Messire Battista..."

"First: Ten slabs best red, seven by 15, by one third,
"Eight ditto, good red, 15 by three by one,
"Six of same, 15 by one by one.

•Eight columns 15 by three and one third
etc... with carriage, danars 151
"Monseigneur:
"Madame Isotta has had me write today about Sr. Galeazzo's
"daughter. The man who said young pullets make thin soup,
"knew what he was talking about. We went to see the girl the
"other day, for all the good that did, and she denied the whole
"matter and kept her end up without losing her temper. I
"think Madame Ixotta very nearly exhausted the matter. *Mi*
"*pare che avea decto hogni chossia.* All the children are well.
"Where you are everyone is pleased and happy because of
"your taking the chateau here we are the reverse as you might
"say drifting without a rudder. Madame Lucrezia has prob-
"ably, or should have, written to you, I suppose you have the
"letter by now. Everyone wants to be remembered to you.
21 Dec. D. de M."
"... *sagramoro* to put up the derricks. There is a supply of
"beams at..."

"Magnificent Lord with due reverence:
"Messire Malatesta is well and asks for you every day. He
"is so much pleased with his pony, It wd. take me a month
"to write you all the fun he gets out of that pony. I want to
"again remind you to write to Georgio Rambottom or to his
"boss to fix up that wall to the little garden that madame Isotta
"uses, for it is all flat on the ground now as I have already told
"him a lot of times, for all the good that does, so I am writing
"to your lordship in the matter I have done all that I can, for
"all the good that does as noboddy hear can do anything
"without you.
"your faithful
Lunarda da Palla.
20 Dec. 1454."

"... gone over it with all the foremen and engineers. And about "the silver for the small medal..."

"*Magnifice ac poten...*
        "because the walls of..."
"*Malatesta de Malatestis ad Magnificum Dominum Patremque "suum.*

"Ex^{so} D^{no} et D^{no} sin D^{no} Sigismundum Pandolfi Filium
        "Malatestis Capitan General

"Magnificent and Exalted Lord and Father in especial my "lord with due recommendation: your letter has been pre-"sented to me by Gentilino da Gradara and with it the bay "pony (ronzino baiectino) the which you have sent me, and "which appears in my eyes a fine caparison'd charger, upon "which I intend to learn all there is to know about riding, in "consideration of yr. paternal affection for which I thank "your excellency thus briefly and pray you continue to hold "me in this esteem notifying you by the bearer of this that "we are all in good health, as I hope and desire your Ex^{et} "Lordship is also: with continued remembrance I remain
        "Your son and servant
                MALATESTA DE MALATESTIS.
        *Given in Rimini, this the 22nd day of December
                anno domini 1454"*
                (*in the sixth year of his age*)

"ILLUSTRIOUS PRINCE:
    "Unfitting as it is that I should offer counsels to Hannibal..."
"*Magnifice ac potens domine, domini mi singularissime,*

112

"*humili recomendatione permissa* etc. This to advise your
"M^gt Ld^shp how the second load of Veronese marble has
"finally got here, after being held up at Ferrara with no end
"of fuss and botheration, the whole of it having been there
"unloaded.

"I learned how it happened, and it has cost a few florins to
"get back the said load which had been seized for the skipper's
"debt and defalcation; he having fled when the lighter was
"seized. But that Y^r M^gt LD^shp may not lose the moneys
"paid out on his account I have had the lighter brought here
"and am holding it, against his arrival. If not we still have
"the lighter.

"As soon as the Xmas fêtes are over I will have the stone
"floor laid in the sacresty, for which the stone is already cut.
"The wall of the building is finished and I shall now get the
"roof on.

"We have not begun putting new stone into the martyr
"chapel; first because the heavy frosts wd. certainly spoil
"the job; secondly because the aliofants aren't yet here and
"one can't get the measurements for the cornice to the columns
"that are to rest on the aliofants.

"They are doing the stairs to your room in the castle... I
"have had Messire Antonio degli Atti's court paved and the
"stone benches put in it.

"Ottavian is illuminating the bull. I mean the bull for the
"chapel. All the stone-cutters are waiting for spring weather
"to start work again.

"The tomb is all done except part of the lid, and as soon as
"Messire Agostino gets back from Cesena I will see that he
"finishes it, ever recommending me to y^r M^gt Ld^shp

"believe me y^r faithful
PETRUS GENARIIS."

113

That's what they found in the post-bag
And some more of it to the effect that
      he "lived and ruled"

"et amava perdutamente Ixotta degli Atti"
e "ne fu degna"
        "constans in proposito
"Placuit oculis principis
"pulchra aspectu"
"populo grata (Italiaeque decus)
"and built a temple so full of pagan works"
       i. e. Sigismund
and in the style "Past ruin'd Latium"
The filagree hiding the gothic,
      with a touch of rhetoric in the whole
And the old sarcophagi,
      such as lie, smothered in grass, by San Vitale.

CANTO XIII

Kung walked
      by the dynastic temple
and into the cedar grove,
      and then out by the lower river,
And with him Khieu Tchi
      and Tian the low speaking
And "we are unknown," said Kung,
"You will take up charioteering?
      "Then you will become known,
"Or perhaps I should take up charioteering, or archery?
"Or the practice of public speaking?"
And Tseu-lou said, "I would put the defences in order,"

And Khieu said, "If I were lord of a province
I would put it in better order than this is."
And Tchi said, "I would prefer a small mountain temple,
"With order in the observances,
            with a suitable performance of the ritual,"
And Tian said, with his hand on the strings of his lute
The low sounds continuing
            after his hand left the strings,
And the sound went up like smoke, under the leaves,
And he looked after the sound:
            "The old swimming hole,
"And the boys flopping off the planks,
"Or sitting in the underbrush playing mandolins."
            And Kung smiled upon all of them equally.
And Thseng-sie desired to know:
            "Which had answered correctly?"
And Kung said, "They have all answered correctly,
"That is to say, each in his nature."
And Kung raised his cane against Yuan Jang,
            Yuan Jang being his elder,
For Yuan Jang sat by the roadside pretending to
            be receiving wisdom.
And Kung said
            "You old fool, come out of it,
"Get up and do something useful."
            And Kung said
"Respect a child's faculties
"From the moment it inhales the clear air,
"But a man of fifty who knows nothing
            Is worthy of no respect."
And "When the prince has gathered about him
"All the savants and artists, his riches will be fully employed."

And Kung said, and wrote on the bo leaves:
        If a man have not order within him
He can not spread order about him;
And if a man have not order within him
His family will not act with due order;
        And if the prince have not order within him
He can not put order in his dominions.
And Kung gave the words "order"
and "brotherly deference"
And said nothing of the "life after death."
And he said
        "Anyone can run to excesses,
"It is easy to shoot past the mark,
"It is hard to stand firm in the middle."

And they said: If a man commit murder
        Should his father protect him, and hide him?
And Kung said:
        He should hide him.

And Kung gave his daughter to Kong-Tchang
        Although Kong-Tchang was in prison.
And he gave his niece to Nan-Young
        although Nan-Young was out of office.
And Kung said "Wan ruled with moderation,
        "In his day the State was well kept,
"And even I can remember
"A day when the historians left blanks in their writings,
"I mean for things they didn't know,
"But that time seems to be passing.
A day when the historians left blanks in their writings,
But that time seems to be passing."

And Kung said, "Without character you will
      "be unable to play on that instrument
"Or to execute the music fit for the Odes.
"The blossoms of the apricot
      "blow from the east to the west,
"And I have tried to keep them from falling."

from CANTO XIV

The slough of unamiable liars,
      bog of stupidities,
malevolent stupidities, and stupidities,
the soil living pus, full of vermin,
dead maggots begetting live maggots,
      slum owners,
usurers squeezing crab-lice, pandars to authority,
pets-de-loup, sitting on piles of stone books,
obscuring the texts with philology,
      hiding them under their persons,
the air without refuge of silence,
      the drift of lice, teething,
and above it the mouthing of orators,
      the arse-belching of preachers.
      And Invidia,
the corruptio, fœtor, fungus,
liquid animals, melted ossifications,
slow rot, fœtid combustion,
      chewed cigar-butts, without dignity, without tragedy,
. . . . .m Episcopus, waving a condom full of black-beetles,
monopolists, obstructors of knowledge.
      obstructors of distribution.

CANTO XVII

So that the vines burst from my fingers
And the bees weighted with pollen
Move heavily in the vine-shoots:
      chirr—chirr—chir-rikk—a purring sound,
And the birds sleepily in the branches.
      ZAGREUS! IO ZAGREUS!
With the first pale-clear of the heaven
And the cities set in their hills,
And the goddess of the fair knees
Moving there, with the oak-wood behind her,
The green slope, with white hounds
      leaping about her;
And thence down to the creek's mouth, until evening,
Flat water before me,
      and the trees growing in water,
Marble trunks out of stillness,
On past the palazzi,
      in the stillness,
The light now, not of the sun.
      Chrysophrase,
And the water green clear, and blue clear;
On, to the great cliffs of amber.
      Between them,
Cave of Nerea,
   she like a great shell curved,
And the boat drawn without sound,
Without odour of ship-work,
Nor bird-cry, nor any noise of wave moving,
Nor splash of porpoise, nor any noise of wave moving,
Within her cave, Nerea,
      she like a great shell curved

In the suavity of the rock,
                    cliff green-gray in the far,
In the near, the gate-cliffs of amber,
And the wave
                    green clear, and blue clear,
And the cave salt-white, and glare-purple,
                    cool, porphyry smooth,
                    the rock sea-worn.
No gull-cry, no sound of porpoise,
Sand as of malachite, and no cold there,
                    the light not of the sun.

Zagreus, feeding his panthers,
                    the turf clear as on hills under light.
And under the almond-trees, gods,
                    with them, *choros nympharum*. Gods,
Hermes and Athene,
                    As shaft of compass,
Between them, trembled—
To the left is the place of fauns,
                    sylva nympharum;
The low wood, moor-scrub,
                    the doe, the young spotted deer,
                    leap up through the broom-plants,
                    as dry leaf amid yellow.
And by one cut of the hills,
                    the great alley of Memnons.
Beyond, sea, crests seen over dune
Night sea churning shingle,
To the left, the alley of cypress.
                    A boat came,
One man holding her sail,
Guiding her with oar caught over gunwale, saying:

"There, in the forest of marble,
"the stone trees—out of water—
"the arbours of stone—
"marble leaf, over leaf,
"silver, steel over steel,
"silver beaks rising and crossing,
"prow set against prow,
"stone, ply over ply,
"the gilt beams flare of an evening"
Borso, Carmagnola, the men of craft, *i vitrei*,
Thither, at one time, time after time,
And the waters richer than glass,
Bronze gold, the blaze over the silver,
Dye-pots in the torch-light,
The flash of wave under prows,
And the silver beaks rising and crossing.
   Stone trees, white and rose-white in the darkness,
Cypress there by the towers,
   Drift under hulls in the night.

   "In the gloom the gold
Gathers the light about it."...

Now supine in burrow, half over-arched bramble,
One eye for the sea, through that peek-hole,
Gray light, with Athene.
Zothar and her elephants, the gold loin-cloth,
The sistrum, shaken, shaken,
   the cohort of her dancers.
And Aletha, by bend of the shore,
   with her eyes seaward,
   and in her hands sea-wrack

120

Salt-bright with the foam.
Koré through the bright meadow,
          with green-gray dust in the grass:
"For this hour, brother of Circe."
Arm laid over my shoulder,
Saw the sun for three days, the sun fulvid,
As a lion lift over sand-plain;
                    and that day,
And for three days, and none after,
Splendour, as the splendour of Hermes,
And shipped thence
                    to the stone place,
Pale white, over water,
              known water,
And the white forest of marble, bent bough over bough,
The pleached arbour of stone,
Thither Borso, when they shot the barbed arrow at him,
And Carmagnola, between the two columns,
Sigismundo, after that wreck in Dalmatia.
          Sunset like the grasshopper flying.

from CANTO XX

          *   *   *   *

And from the floating bodies, the incense
          blue-pale, purple above them.
Shelf of the lotophagoi,
Aerial, cut in the æther.
                         Reclining,
With silver spilla,
The ball as of melted amber, coiled, caught up, and turned.
Lotophagoi of the suave nails, quiet, scornful,

Voce-profondo:
    "Feared neither death nor pain for this beauty;
If harm, harm to ourselves."
And beneath: the clear bones, far down,
Thousand on thousand.
    "What gain with Odysseus,
"They that died in the whirlpool
"And after many vain labours,
"Living by stolen meat, chained to the rowingbench,
"That he should have a great fame
        "And lie by night with the goddess?
"Their names are not written in bronze
        "Nor their rowing sticks set with Elpenor's;
"Nor have they mound by sea-bord.
        "That saw never the olives under Spartha
"With the leaves green and then not green,
        "The click of light in their branches;
"That saw not the bronze hall nor the ingle
"Nor lay there with the queen's waiting maids,
"Nor had they Circe to couch-mate, Circe Titania,
"Nor had they meats of Kalüpso
"Or her silk skirts brushing their thighs.
"Give! What were they given?
                    Ear-wax.
"Poison and ear-wax,
            and a salt grave by the bull-field,
"*neson amumona*, their heads like sea crows in the foam,
"Black splotches, sea-weed under lightning;
"Canned beef of Apollo, ten cans for a boat load."
Ligur' aoide.
· · ·

from CANTO XXV

. . .

...because of the stink of the dungeons. 1344.
1409... since the most serene Doge can scarce
stand upright in his bedroom...
                        vadit pars, two gross lire
stone stair, 1415, for pulchritude of the palace

                        254 da parte
                        de non 23
                        4 non sincere
Which is to say: they built out over the arches
and the palace hangs there in the dawn, the mist,
in that dimness,
or as one rows in from past the murazzi
the barge slow after moon-rise
and the voice sounding under the sail.
Mist gone.
        And Sulpicia
green shoot now, and the wood
white under new cortex
"as the sculptor sees the form in the air
        before he sets hand to mallet,
"and as he sees the in, and the through,
                        the four sides
"not the one face to the painter"
As ivory uncorrupted:
                "Pone metum Cerinthe"
Lay there, the long soft grass,
        and the flute lay there by her thigh,
Sulpicia, the fauns, twig-strong,
                gathered about her;

The fluid, over the grass
Zephyrus, passing through her,
                    "deus nec laedit amantes."
Hic mihi dies sanctus;
And from the stone pits, the heavy voices,
Heavy sound:
                    "Sero, sero...
"Nothing we made, we set nothing in order,
"Neither house nor the carving,
"And what we thought had been thought for too long;
"Our opinion not opinion in evil
"But opinion borne for too long.
"We have gathered a sieve full of water."
And from the comb of reeds, came notes and the chorus
Moving, the young fauns: Pone metum,
Metum, nec deus laedit.

And as after the form, the shadow,
Noble forms, lacking life, that bolge, that valley
the dead words keeping form,
and the cry: Civis Romanus.
The clear air, dark, dark,
The dead concepts, never the solid, the blood rite,
The vanity of Ferrara;

Clearer than shades, in the hill road
Springing in cleft of the rock: Phaethusa
There as she came among them,
Wine in the smoke-faint throat,
Fire gleam under smoke of the mountain,
Even there by meadows of Phlegethon
And against this the flute: pone metum.

Fading, that they carried their guts before them,
And thought then: the deathless,
Form, forms and renewal, gods held in the air,
Forms seen, and then clearness,
Bright void, without image, Napishtim,
Casting his gods back into the νοῦς.

"as the sculptor sees the form in the air...
"as glass seen under water,
"King Otreus, my father..."
and saw the waves taking form as crystal,
notes as facets of air,
and the mind there, before them, moving,
so that notes needed not move.

. . .

from CANTO XXX

Compleynt, compleynt I hearde upon a day,
Artemis singing, Artemis, Artemis
Agaynst Pity lifted her wail:
Pity causeth the forests to fail,
Pity slayeth my nymphs,
Pity spareth so many an evil thing.
Pity befouleth April,
Pity is the root and the spring.
Now if no fayre creature followeth me
It is on account of Pity,
It is on account that Pity forbideth them slaye.
All things are made foul in this season,
This is the reason, none may seek purity
Having for foulnesse pity

And things growne awry;
No more do my shaftes fly
To slay. Nothing is now clean slayne
But rotteth away.

In Paphos, on a day
                    I also heard:
...goeth not with young Mars to playe
But she hath pity on a doddering fool,
She tendeth his fyre,
She keepeth his embers warm.

Time is the evil. Evil.
                    A day, and a day
Walked the young Pedro baffled,
                    a day and a day
After Ignez was murdered.
Came the Lords in Lisboa
                    a day, and a day
In homage. Seated there
                    dead eyes,
Dead hair under the crown,
The King still young there beside her.
. . .

from CANTO XXXVI

A lady asks me
            I speak in season
She seeks reason for an affect, wild often
That is so proud he hath Love for a name
Who denys it can hear the truth now

126

Wherefore I speak to the present knowers
Having no hope that low-hearted
     Can bring sight to such reason
Be there not natural demonstration
        I have no will to try proof-bringing
Or say where it hath birth
What is its virtu and power
Its being and every moving
Or delight whereby 'tis called "to love"
Or if man can show it to sight.

Where memory liveth,
       it takes its state
Formed like a diafan from light on shade
Which shadow cometh of Mars and remaineth
Created, having a name sensate,
Custom of the soul,
       will from the heart;

Cometh from a seen form which being understood
Taketh locus and remaining in the intellect possible
Wherein hath he neither weight nor still-standing,
Descendeth not by quality but shineth out
Himself his own effect unendingly
Not in delight but in the being aware
Nor can he leave his true likeness otherwhere.

He is not vertu but cometh of that perfection
Which is so postulate not by the reason
But 'tis felt, I say.
Beyond salvation, holdeth his judging force
Deeming intention to be reason's peer and mate,

Poor in discernment, being thus weakness' friend

Often his power cometh on death in the end,
Be it withstayed
  and so swinging counterweight.
Not that it were natural opposite, but only
Wry'd a bit from the perfect,
Let no man say love cometh from chance
Or hath not established lordship
Holding his power even though
  Memory hath him no more.

Cometh he to be
  when the will
From overplus
Twisteth out of natural measure,
Never adorned with rest Moveth he changing colour
Either to laugh or weep
Contorting the face with fear
  resteth but a little
Yet shall ye see of him That he is most often
With folk who deserve him
And his strange quality sets sighs to move
Willing man look into that forméd trace in his mind
And with such uneasiness as rouseth the flame.
Unskilled can not form his image,
He himself moveth not, drawing all to his stillness,
Neither turneth about to seek his delight
Nor yet to seek out proving
Be it so great or so small.

He draweth likeness and hue from like nature
So making pleasure more certain in seeming

Nor can stand hid in such nearness,
Beautys be darts tho' not savage
Skilled from such fear a man follows
Deserving spirit, that pierceth.
Nor is he known from his face
But taken in the white light that is allness
Toucheth his aim

Who heareth, seeth not form
But is led by its emanation.
Being divided, set out from colour,
Disjunct in mid darkness
Grazeth the light, one moving by other,
Being divided, divided from all falsity
Worthy of trust
From him alone mercy proceedeth.

Go, song, surely thou mayest
Whither it please thee
For so art thou ornate that thy reasons
Shall be praised from thy understanders,
With others hast thou no will to make company.
. . .

CANTO XXXVIII

> *il duol che sopra Senna
> Induce, falseggiando la moneta.*
> Paradiso XIX, 118.

An' that year Metevsky went over to America del Sud
(and the Pope's manners were so like Mr Joyce's,
got that way in the Vatican, weren't like that before)

Marconi knelt in the ancient manner
           like Jimmy Walker sayin' his prayers.
His Holiness expressed a polite curiosity
           as to how His Excellency had chased those
electric shakes through the a'mosphere.
           Lucrezia
Wanted a rabbit's foot,
           and he, Metevsky said to the one side
(three children, five abortions and died of the last)
           he said: the other boys got more munitions
(thus cigar-makers whose work is highly repetitive
can perform the necessary operations almost automatically
and at the same time listen to readers who are hired
for the purpose of providing mental entertainment while they
work; Dexter Kimball 1929.)

Don't buy until you can get ours.
And he went over the border
           and he said to the other side:
The *other* side has more munitions. Don't buy
           until you can get ours.
And Akers made a large profit and imported gold into Eng-
           land
Thus increasing gold imports.
           The gentle reader has heard this before.
And that year Mr Whitney
Said how useful short sellin' was,
           We suppose he meant to the brokers
And no one called him a liar.
And two Afghans came to Geneva
To see if they cd. get some guns cheap,
As they had heard about someone's disarming.

And the secretary of the something
Made some money from oil wells
                    (In the name of God the Most Glorious Mr D'Arcy
is empowered to scratch through the sub-soil of Persia
until fifty years from this date...)
Mr Mellon went over to England
and that year Mr Wilson had prostatitis
And there was talk of a new Messiah
(that must have been a bit sooner)
And her Ladyship cut down Jenny's allowance
Because of that bitch Agot Ipswich
And that year (that wd. be 20 or 18 years sooner)
They began to kill 'em by millions
Because of a louse in Berlin
                    and a greasy basturd in Ausstria
By name François Giuseppe.

"Will there be war?" "No, Miss Wi'let,
"On account of bizschniz relations."
                    Said the soap and bones dealer in May 1914
And Mr Gandhi thought:
                    if we don't buy any cotton
And at the same time don't buy any guns......
Monsieur Untel was not found at the Jockey Club
...but was, later, found in Japan
And So-and-So had shares in Mitsui.
"The wood (walnut) will always be wanted for gunstocks"
And they put up a watch factory outside Muscou
And the watches kept time.... Italian marshes
been waiting since Tiberius' time...
"Marry" said Beebe, "how do the fish live in the sea."
Rivera, the Spanish dictator, dictated that the

131

Infante was physically unfit to inherIt...
                    gothic type still used in Vienna
because the old folks are used to that type.
                                        And Schlossmann
suggested that I stay there in Vienna
As stool-pigeon against the Anschluss
            Because the Ausstrians needed a Buddha
(Seay, brother, I leev et tuh yew!)
The white man who made the tempest in Baluba
Der im Baluba das Gewitter gemacht hat...
                    they spell words with a drum beat,
"The country is overbrained" said the hungarian nobleman
in 1923. Kosouth (Ku' shoot) used, I understand
To sit in a café—all done by conversation—
It was all done by conversation,
            possibly because one repeats the point when conversing:
"Vienna contains a mixture of races."
                    wd. I stay and be Bhudd-ha?
"They are accustomed to having an Emperor. They must have
Something to worship. (1927)"
But their humour about losing the Tyrol?
Their humour is not quite so broad.
The ragged arab spoke with Frobenius and told him
The names of 3000 plants.
                    Bruhl found some languages full of detail
Words that half mimic action; but
generalization is beyond them, a white dog is
not, let us say, a dog like a black dog.
Do not happen, Romeo and Juliet...unhappily
I have lost the cutting but apparently
such things do still happen, he
suicided outside her door while

the family was preparing her body for burial,
and she knew that this was the case.

Green, black, December. Said Mr Blodgett:
"Sewing machines will never come into general use."

"I have of course never said that the cash is constant"
(Douglas) and in fact the population (Britain 1914)
was left with 800 millions of '*deposits*'
after all the cash had been drawn, and
these deposits were satisfied by the
               printing of treasury notes.
A factory
has also another aspect, which we call the financial aspect
It gives people the power to buy (wages, dividends
which are power to buy) but it is also the cause of prices
or values, financial, I mean financial values
It pays workers, and pays *for* material.
What it pays in wages and dividends
stays fluid, as power to buy, and this power is less,
per forza, damn blast your intellex, is less
than the total payments made by the factory
(as wages, dividends AND payments for raw material
bank charges etcetera
and all, that is the whole, that is the total
of these is added into the total of prices
caused by that factory, any damn factory
and there is and must be therefore a clog
and the power to purchase can never
(under the present system) catch up with
prices at large,

133

and the light became so bright and so blindin'
in this layer of paradise
that the mind of man was bewildered.
Said Herr Krupp (1842): guns are a merchandise
I approach them from the industrial end,
I approach them from the technical side,
1847 orders from Paris and Egypt....
orders from the Crimea,
Order of Pietro il Grande,
and a Command in the Legion of Honour...
500 to St Petersburg and 300 to Napoleon Barbiche
from Creusot. At Sadowa
Austria had some Krupp cannon;
Prussia had some Krupp cannon.
"The Emperor ('68) is deeply in'erested in yr. catalogue
and in yr. services to humanity"

(signed) Leboeuf
who was a relative of Monsieur Schneider
1900 fifty thousand operai,
53 thousand cannon, about half for his country,
Bohlem und Halbach,
Herr Schneider of Creusot
Twin arse with one belly.
Eugene, Adolf and Alfred "more money from guns than from
tractiles"
Eugene was sent to the deputies;
(Soane et Loire) to the Deputies, minister;
Later rose to be minister,
"guns coming from anywhere,
but appropriations from the Chambers of Parliaments"
In 1874 recd. license for free exportation
Adopted by 22 nations

1885/1900 produced ten thousand cannon
to 1914, 34 thousand
one half of them sent out of the country
always in the chamber of deputies, always a conservative,
Schools, churches, orspitals fer the workin' man
Sand piles fer the children.
Opposite the Palace of the Schneiders
            Arose the monument to Herr Henri
Chantiers de la Gironde, Bank of the Paris Union,
The franco-japanese bank
            François de Wendel, Robert Protot
To friends and enemies of tomorrow
"the most powerful union is doubtless
            that of the Comité des Forges,"
"And God take your living" said Hawkwood
15 million: Journal des Débats
30 million paid to Le Temps
Eleven for the Echo de Paris
Polloks on Schneider patents
Our bank has bought us
            a lot of shares in Mitsui
Who arm 50 divisions, who keep up the Japanese army
and they are destined to have a large future
"faire passer ces affaires
            avant celles de la nation."

CANTO XLV

With *Usura*
With usura hath no man a house of good stone
each block cut smooth and well fitting

that design might cover their face,
with usura
hath no man a painted paradise on his church wall
harpes et luthes
or where virgin receiveth message
and halo projects from incision,
with usura
seeth no man Gonzaga his heirs and his concubines
no picture is made to endure nor to live with
but it is made to sell and sell quickly
with usura, sin against nature,
is thy bread ever more of stale rags
is thy bread dry as paper,
with no mountain wheat, no strong flour
with usura the line grows thick
with usura is no clear demarcation
and no man can find site for his dwelling.
Stone cutter is kept from his stone
weaver is kept from his loom
WITH USURA
wool comes not to market
sheep bringeth no gain with usura
Usura is a murrain, usura
blunteth the needle in the maid's hand
and stoppeth the spinner's cunning. Pietro Lombardo
came not by usura
Duccio came not by usura
nor Pier della Francesca; Zuan Bellin' not by usura
nor was 'La Calunnia' painted.
Came not by usura Angelico; came not Ambrogio Praedis,
Came no church of cut stone signed: *Adamo me fecit.*
Not by usura St Trophime

Not by usura Saint Hilaire,
Usura rusteth the chisel
It rusteth the craft and the craftsman
It gnaweth the thread in the loom
None learneth to weave gold in her pattern;
Azure hath a canker by usura; cramoisi is unbroidered
Emerald findeth no Memling
Usura slayeth the child in the womb
It stayeth the young man's courting
It hath brought palsey to bed, lyeth
between the young bride and her bridegroom
                     CONTRA NATURAM
They have brought whores for Eleusis
Corpses are set to banquet
at behest of usura.

CANTO XLVII

Who even dead, yet hath his mind entire!
This sound came in the dark
First must thou go the road
                          to hell
And to the bower of Ceres' daughter Proserpine,
Through overhanging dark, to see Tiresias,
Eyeless that was, a shade, that is in hell
So full of knowing that the beefy men know less than he,
Ere thou come to thy road's end.
                 Knowledge the shade of a shade,
Yet must thou sail after knowledge
Knowing less than drugged beasts. *phtheggometha
thasson*

φθεγγώμεθα θᾶσσον
        The small lamps drift in the bay
And the sea's claw gathers them.
Neptunus drinks after neap-tide.
Tamuz! Tamuz!!
The red flame going seaward.
          By this gate art thou measured.
From the long boats they have set lights in the water,
The sea's claw gathers them outward.
Scilla's dogs snarl at the cliff's base,
The white teeth gnaw in under the crag,
But in the pale night the small lamps float seaward
                Τυ Διώνα
                TU DIONA

Καὶ Μοῖραι τ' Ἄδονιν
KAI MOIRAI' T' ADONIN
The sea is streaked red with Adonis,
The lights flicker red in small jars.
Wheat shoots rise new by the altar,
        flower from the swift seed.
Two span, two span to a woman,
Beyond that she believes not. Nothing is of any importance.
To that is she bent, her intention
To that art thou called ever turning intention,
Whether by night the owl-call, whether by sap in shoot,
Never idle, by no means by no wiles intermittent
Moth is called over mountain
The bull runs blind on the sword, *naturans*
To the cave art thou called, Odysseus,
By Molü hast thou respite for a little,
By Molü art thou freed from the one bed
        that thou may'st return to another

The stars are not in her counting,
          To her they are but wandering holes.
Begin thy plowing
When the Pleiades go down to their rest,
Begin thy plowing
40 days are they under seabord,
Thus do in fields by seabord
And in valleys winding down toward the sea.
When the cranes fly high
          think of plowing.
By this gate art thou measured
Thy day is between a door and a door
Two oxen are yoked for plowing
Or six in the hill field
White bulk under olives, a score for drawing down stone,
Here the mules are gabled with slate on the hill road.
Thus was it in time.
And the small stars now fall from the olive branch,
Forked shadow falls dark on the terrace
More black than the floating martin
          that has no care for your presence,
His wing-print is black on the roof tiles
And the print is gone with his cry.
So light is thy weight on Tellus
Thy notch no deeper indented
Thy weight less than the shadow
Yet hast thou gnawed through the mountain,
          Scylla's white teeth less sharp.
Hast thou found a nest softer than cunnus
Or hast thou found better rest
Hast'ou a deeper planting, doth thy death year
Bring swifter shoot?
Hast thou entered more deeply the mountain?

The light has entered the cave. Io! Io!
The light has gone down into the cave,
Splendour on splendour!
By prong have I entered these hills:
That the grass grow from my body,
That I hear the roots speaking together,
The air is new on my leaf,
The forked boughs shake with the wind.
Is Zephyrus more light on the bough, Apeliota
more light on the almond branch?
By this door have I entered the hill.
Falleth,
Adonis falleth.
Fruit cometh after. The small lights drift out with the tide,
sea's claw has gathered them outward,
Four banners to every flower
The sea's claw draws the lamps outward.
Think thus of thy plowing
When the seven stars go down to their rest
Forty days for their rest, by seabord
And in valleys that wind down toward the sea

Καὶ Μοῖραι᾽ τ᾽ Ἄδονιν
KAI MOIRAI᾽ T᾽ ADONIN

When the almond bough puts forth its flame,
When the new shoots are brought to the altar,

Τυ Διώνα, Καὶ Μοῖραι
TU DIONA, KAI MOIRAI

Καὶ Μοῖραι᾽ τ᾽ Ἄδονιν
KAI MOIRAI᾽ T᾽ ADONIN

            that hath the gift of healing,
that hath the power over wild beasts.

140

CANTO XLIX

For the seven lakes, and by no man these verses:
Rain; empty river; a voyage,
Fire from frozen cloud, heavy rain in the twilight
Under the cabin roof was one lantern.
The reeds are heavy; bent;
and the bamboos speak as if weeping.

Autumn moon; hills rise about lakes
against sunset
Evening is like a curtain of cloud,
a blurr above ripples; and through it
sharp long spikes of the cinnamon,
a cold tune amid reeds.
Behind hill the monk's bell
borne on the wind.
Sail passed here in April; may return in October
Boat fades in silver; slowly;
Sun blaze alone on the river.

Where wine flag catches the sunset
Sparse chimneys smoke in the cross light

Comes then snow scur on the river
And a world is covered with jade
Small boat floats like a lanthorn,
The flowing water clots as with cold. And at San Yin
they are a people of leisure

Wild geese swoop to the sand-bar,
Clouds gather about the hole of the window

Broad water; geese line out with the autumn
Rooks clatter over the fishermen's lanthorns,

A light moves on the north sky line;
where the young boys prod stones for shrimp.
In seventeen hundred came Tsing to these hill lakes.
A light moves on the south sky line.

State by creating riches shd. thereby get into debt?
This is infamy; this is Geryon.
This canal goes still to TenShi
though the old king built it for pleasure

KEI	MEN	RAN	KEI
KIU	MAN	MAN	KEI
JITSU	GETSU	KO	KWA
TAN	FUKU	TAN	KAI

Sun up; work
sundown; to rest
dig well and drink of the water
dig field; eat of the grain
Imperial power is? and to us what is it?

The fourth; the dimension of stillness.
And the power over wild beasts.

CANTO LI

Shines
in the mind of heaven God
who made it

more than the sun
in our eye.
Fifth element; mud; said Napoleon
With usury has no man a good house
made of stone, no paradise on his church wall
With usury the stone cutter is kept from his stone
the weaver is kept from his loom by usura
Wool does not come into market
the peasant does not eat his own grain
the girl's needle goes blunt in her hand
The looms are hushed one after another
ten thousand after ten thousand
Duccio was not by usura
Nor was 'La Calunnia' painted.
Neither Ambrogio Praedis nor Angelico
had their skill by usura
Nor St Trophime its cloisters;
Nor St Hilaire its proportion.
Usury rusts the man and his chisel
It destroys the craftsman, destroying craft;
Azure is caught with cancer. Emerald comes to no Memling
Usury kills the child in the womb
And breaks short the young man's courting
Usury brings age into youth; it lies between the bride
and the bridegroom
Usury is against Nature's increase.
Whores for Eleusis;
Under usury no stone is cut smooth
Peasant has no gain from his sheep herd
          Blue dun; number 2 in most rivers
for dark days, when it is cold
A starling's wing will give you the colour

or duck widgeon, if you take feather from under the wing
Let the body be of blue fox fur, or a water rat's
or grey squirrel's. Take this with a portion of mohair
and a cock's hackle for legs.
12th of March to 2nd of April
Hen pheasant's feather does for a fly,
green tail, the wings flat on the body
Dark fur from a hare's ear for a body
a green shaded partridge feather
                grizzled yellow cock's hackle
green wax; harl from a peacock's tail
bright lower body; about the size of pin
the head should be. can be fished from seven a.m.
till eleven; at which time the brown marsh fly comes on.
As long as the brown continues, no fish will take Granham

That hath the light of the doer, as it were
a form cleaving to it.
Deo similis quodam modo
hic intellectus adeptus
Grass; nowhere out of place. Thus speaking in Königsberg
Zwischen die Volkern erzielt wird
a modus vivendi.
circling in eddying air; in a hurry;
the 12: close eyed in the oily wind
these were the regents; and a sour song from the folds
                of his belly
sang Geryone; I am the help of the aged;
I pay men to talk peace;
Mistress of many tongues; merchant of chalcedony
I am Geryon twin with usura,
You who have lived in a stage set.

A thousand were dead in his folds;
in the eel-fishers basket
Time was of the League of Cambrai:

from CANTO LIII

Yeou taught men to break branches
Seu Gin set up the stage and taught barter,
        taught the knotting of cords
Fou Hi taught men to grow barley
        2837 ante Christum
and they know still where his tomb is
by the high cypress between the strong walls.
the FIVE grains, said Chin Nong, that are
        wheat, rice, millet, *gros blé* and chic peas
and made a plough that is used five thousand years
Moved his court then to Kio-feou-hien
held market at mid-day
'bring what we have not here', wrote an herbal
Souan Yen bagged fifteen tigers
        made signs out of bird tracks
Hoang Ti contrived the making of bricks
and his wife started working the silk worms,
        money was in days of Hoang Ti.
He measured the length of Syrinx
        of the tubes to make tune for song
Twenty-six (that was) eleven ante Christum
        had four wives and 25 males of his making
His tomb is today in Kiao-Chan
Ti Ko set his scholars to fitting words to their music
        is buried in Tung Kieou

This was in the twenty-fifth century a.c.
　　　　YAO like the sun and rain,
saw what star is at solstice
saw what star marks mid summer
YU, leader of waters,
　　　　black earth is fertile, wild silk still is from Shantung
Ammassi, to the provinces,
　　　　let his men pay tithes in kind.
'Siu-tcheou province to pay in earth of five colours
Pheasant plumes from the Yu-chan of mountains
Yu-chan to pay sycamores
　　　　of this wood are lutes made
Ringing stones from Se-choui river
and grass that is called Tsing-mo' or μῶλυ,
Chun to the spirit Chang Ti, of heaven
moving the sun and stars
　　　　que vos vers expriment vos intentions,
　　　　et que la musique conforme

YAO

CHUN　　　　　　KAO-YAO

YU

146

For years no waters came, no rain fell
        for the Emperor Tching Tang
grain scarce, prices rising
so that in 1766 Tching Tang opened the copper mine (ante
                                              Christum)
made discs with square holes in their middles
        and gave these to the people
wherewith they might buy grain
                        where there was grain
The silos were emptied
7 years of sterility
                der im Baluba das Gewitter gemacht hat
Tching prayed on the mountain and
        wrote MAKE IT NEW
on his bath tub
        Day by day make it new
cut underbrush,
pile the logs
keep it growing.
Died Tching aged years an hundred,
in the 13th of his reign.
        "We are up, Hia is down."
Immoderate love of women
Immoderate love of riches,
Cared for parades and huntin'.
        Chang Ti above alone rules.
Tang not stinting of praise:
        Consider their sweats, the people's
If you wd/ sit calm on throne.

Thus came Kang to be Emperor/.
White horses with sorrel manes in the court yard.
      "I am pro-Tcheou" said Confucius
      "I am" said Confutzius "pro-Tcheou in politics"
Wen-wang and Wu-wang had sage men, strong as bears
      Said young Kang-wang:
                        Help me to keep the peace!
Your ancestors have come one by one under our rule
                           for our rule.
Honour to Chao-Kong the surveyor.
      Let his name last 3000 years
Gave each man land for his labour
         not by plough-land alone
But for keeping of silk worms
        Reforested the mulberry groves
        Set periodical markets
Exchange brought abundance, the prisons were empty.
"Yao and Chun have returned"
        sang the farmers
"Peace and abundance bring virtue." I am
      'pro-Tcheou' said Confucius five centuries later.
With his mind on this age.

Then Kungfutseu was made minister and moved promptly
                    against T. C. Mao
     and had him beheaded
that was false and crafty of heart
       a tough tongue that flowed with deceit
A man who remembered evil and was complacent in doing it.
LOU rose. Tsi sent girls to destroy it
      Kungfutseu retired

At Tching someone said:
                    there is man with Yao's forehead
Cao's neck and the shoulders of Tsé Tchin
A man tall as Yu, and he wanders about in front of the
                                                      East gate
            like a dog that has lost his owner.
Wrong, said Confucius, in what he says of those Emperors
            but as to the lost dog, quite correct.
He was seven days foodless in Tchin
            the rest sick and Kung making music
'sang even more than was usual'
Honour to Yng P the bastard
Tchin and Tsai cut off Kung in the desert
            and Tcheou troops alone got him out
            Tsao fell after 25 generations
And Kung cut 3000 odes to 300
Comet from Yng star to Sin star, that is two degrees long
in the 40th year of King Ouang
Died Kung aged 73   *b.c.* 479

Thus of Kung or Confucius, and of 'Hillock' his father
when he was attacking a city
his men had passed under the drop gate
And the warders then dropped it, so Hillock caught
the whole weight on his shoulder, and held till his
last man had got out.
            Of such stock was Kungfutseu.

149

from CANTO LXII

'*Acquit of evil intention*
or inclination to perseverance in error
to correct it with cheerfulness
particularly as to the motives of actions
of the great nations of Europe.'
                    for the planting
and ruling and ordering of New England
from latitude 40° to 48°
TO THE GOVERNOR AND THE COMPANIE
                whereon Thomas Adams
                19th March 1628
18th assistant whereof the said Thomas Adams
                (abbreviated)
Merry Mount become Braintree, a plantation near Weston's
Capn Wollanston's became Merrymount.
            ten head 40 acres at 3/ (shillings) per acre
who lasted 6 years, brewing commenced by the first Henry
            continued by Joseph Adams, his son
at decease left a malting establishment.
Born 1735; 19th Oct. old style; 30th new style John Adams
its emolument gave but a bare scanty subsistence.
'Passion of orthodoxy is fear, Calvinism has no other agent
study of theology
            wd/ involve me in endless altercation
to no purpose, of no design and do no good to
                any man whatsoever...
not less of order than liberty...
            Burke, Gibbon, beautifiers of figures...
middle path, resource of second-rate statesmen...

茶 produced not in Britain:
                              tcha
          tax falls on the colonists.
        Lord North, purblind to the rights of a
continent, eye on a few London merchants...
                    no longer saw redcoat
as brother or as a protector
(Boston about the size of Rapallo)
        scarce 16,000,
              habits of freedom now formed
even among those who scarcely got so far as analysis
so about 9 o'c in the morning Lard Narf wuz bein' impassible
was a light fall of snow in Bastun, in King St.
and the 29th Styschire in Brattle St
Murray's barracks, and in this case was a
              baker's boy ragging the sentinel
so Capn Preston etc/
lower order with billets of wood and 'just roving'
force in fact of a right sez Chawles Fwancis
              at same time, and in Louses of Parleymoot...
so fatal a precision of aim,
                    sojers aiming??
Gent standing in his doorway got 2 balls in the arm
and five deaders 'never Cadmus...' etc
              was more pregnant
patriots need legal advisor
          measures involvin' pro-fessional knowl-edge
BE IT ENACTED / guv-nor council an' house of assembly
          (Blaydon objectin' to form ov these doggymints)
Encourage arts commerce an' farmin'
not suggest anything on my own
              if ever abandoned by administration of England

           and outrage of the soldiery
the bonds of affection be broken
till then let us try cases by law IF by
                snowballs oystershells cinders
                was provocation
                reply was then manslaughter only
in consideration of endocrine human emotions
unuprootable, that is, human emotions—
                merely manslaughter
                brand 'em in hand
but not hang 'em being mere human blighters
                common men like the rest of us
                subjekk to
                                    passions
law not bent to wanton imagination
                            and temper of individuals
mens sine affectu
                that law rules
                that it be
                sine affectu in 1770, Bastun.
Bad law is the worst sort of tyranny. Burke
disputed right to seize lands of the heathen
and give it to any king, If we be feudatory
parliament has no control over us
                We are merely
under the monarch
allegiance is to the king's natural person 'The Spensers'
said Coke, hatched treason denying this
allegiance follows natural, not politic person
are we mere slaves of some other people?

Mercantile temper of Britain
constitution...without appeal to higher powers unwritten
VOTED 92 to 8 against Oliver
            i.e. against king's pay for the judges instead of
                having the wigs paid by the colony
                no jurors wd/ serve
These are the stones of foundation
J. A.'s reply to the Governor
Impeachment of Oliver
These stones we built on

----

from CANTO LXXIV

The enormous tragedy of the dream in the peasant's bent
    shoulders
Manes! Manes was tanned and stuffed,
Thus Ben and la Clara *a Milano*
            by the heels at Milano
That maggots shd/ eat the dead bullock
DIGENES, διγενές, but the twice crucified
                where in history will you find it?
yet say this to the Possum: a bang, not a whimper,
    with a bang not with a whimper,
To build the city of Dioce whose terraces are the colour of
    stars.
The suave eyes, quiet, not scornful,
                    rain also is of the process.
What you depart from is not the way
and olive tree blown white in the wind

washed in the Kiang and Han
what whiteness will you add to this whiteness,
                                          what candor?

--- .

and there was a smell of mint under the tent flaps
especially after the rain
                    and a white ox on the road toward Pisa
                        as if facing the tower,
dark sheep in the drill field and on wet days were clouds
in the mountain as if under the guard roosts.
            A lizard upheld me
                the wild birds wd not eat the white bread
                from Mt Taishan to the sunset
From Carrara stone to the tower
        and this day the air was made open
            for Kuanon of all delights,
                Linus, Cletus, Clement
                            whose prayers,
the great scarab is bowed at the altar
the green light gleams in his shell
plowed in the sacred field and unwound the silk worms early
                                        in tensile
in the light of light is the *virtù*
            "sunt lumina" said Erigena Scotus
                as of Shun on Mt Taishan
and in the hall of the forebears
                    as from the beginning of wonders
the paraclete that was present in Yao, the precision
in Shun the compassionate
in Yu the guider of waters

---.. .

Tempus tacendi, tempus loquendi.
Never inside the country to raise the standard of living
but always abroad to increase the profits of usurers,
                    dixit Lenin,
and gun sales lead to more gun sales
            they do not clutter the market for gunnery
                there is no saturation
Pisa, in the 23rd year of the effort in sight of the tower
and Till was hung yesterday
for murder and rape with trimmings   plus Cholkis
        plus mythology, thought he was Zeus ram or another one
            Hey Snag wots in the bibl'?
            wot are the books ov the bible?
            Name 'em, don't bullshit ME.

- -

            a man on whom the sun has gone down
and the wind came as hamadryas under the sun-beat
                    Vai soli
                            are never alone
amid the slaves learning slavery
            and the dull driven back toward the jungle
            are never alone ῾ΗΛΙΟΝ ΠΕΡΙ῾ΗΛΙΟΝ
                as the light sucks up vapor
                    and the tides follow Lucina
                that had been a hard man in some ways
                a day as a thousand years
as the leopard sat by his water dish;

- -

nor is it for nothing that the chrysalids mate in the air
                              color di luce
green splendour and as the sun thru pale fingers
Lordly men are to earth o'ergiven
               these the companions:
Fordie who wrote of giants
               and William who dreamed of nobility
                  and Jim the comedian singing:
                        "Blarrney castle me darlin'
                        you're nothing now but a StOWne"
and Plarr talking of mathematics
               or Jepson lover of jade
Maurie who wrote historical novels
               and Newbolt who looked twice bathed
                           are to earth o'ergiven.
               And this day the sun was clouded
—"You sit stiller" said Kokka
"if whenever you move something jangles."

----

and Mr Edwards superb green and brown
                  in ward No 4 a jacent benignity,
of the Baluba mask: "doan you tell no one
     I made you that table"
                        methenamine eases the urine
and the greatest is charity
to be found among those who have not observed
                              regulations
          not of course that we advocate—
          and yet petty larceny
          in a regime based on grand larceny

156

might rank as conformity nient' altro
    with justice shall be redeemed
who putteth not out his money on interest
    "in meteyard in weight or in measure"
          XIX Leviticus or
First Thessalonians 4, 11
300 years culture at the mercy of a tack hammer
        thrown thru the roof
Cloud over mountain, mountain over the cloud
I surrender neither the empire nor the temples
                    plural
nor the constitution nor yet the city of Dioce
each one in his god's name
as by Terracina rose from the sea Zephyr behind her
      and from her manner of walking
              as had Anchises
    till the shrine be again white with marble
    till the stone eyes look again seaward
                The wind is part of the process
                The rain is part of the process
and the Pleiades set in her mirror
Kuanon, this stone bringeth sleep;

I don't know how humanity stands it
    with a painted paradise at the end of it
    without a painted paradise at the end of it
the dwarf morning-glory twines round the grass blade
magna NUX animae   with Barabbas and 2 thieves beside me,

----

nox animae magna from the tent under Taishan
amid what was termed the a.h. of the army
the guards holding opinion. As it were to dream of
morticians' daughters raddled but amorous
To study with the white wings of time passing
        is not that our delight
to have friends come from far countries
        is not that pleasure
nor to care that we are untrumpeted?
        filial, fraternal affection is the root of humaneness
        the root of the process
nor are elaborate speeches and slick alacrity.
        employ men in proper season
        not when they are at harvest
        E al Triedro, Cunizza
       e l'altra: "Io son' la Luna."
dry friable earth going from dust to more dust
    grass worn from its root-hold
    is it blacker? was it blacker? Νύξ animae?
    is there a blacker or was it merely San Juan with
        a belly ache writing ad posteros
    in short shall we look for a deeper or is this the
        bottom?

Time is not, Time is the evil, beloved
Beloved the hours βροδοδάκτυλος
        as against the half-light of the window
        with the sea beyond making horizon
le contre-jour the line of the cameo
profile "to carve Achaia"
        a dream passing over the face in the half-light
        Venere, Cytherea "aut Rhodon"

vento ligure, veni
"beauty is difficult" sd/ Mr Beardsley

----

and that certain images be formed in the mind
                    to remain there
                              formato locho
        Arachne mi porta fortuna
to remain there, resurgent eikons
and still in Trastevere
for the deifications of emperors
and the medallions
                    to forge Achaia

Serenely in the crystal jet
            as the bright ball that the fountain tosses
(Verlaine) as diamond clearness
            How soft the wind under Taishan
                    where the sea is remembered
            out of hell, the pit
            out of the dust and glare evil
            Zephyrus / Apeliota
This liquid is certainly a
            property of the mind
nec accidens est   but an element
                              in the mind's make-up
est agens and functions   dust to a fountain pan otherwise
            Hast 'ou seen the rose in the steel dust
                        (or swansdown ever?)
so light is the urging, so ordered the dark petals of iron
we who have passed over Lethe.

from CANTO LXXVI

                    l'ara sul rostro
20 years of the dream
              and the clouds near to Pisa
                    are as good as any in Italy
said the young Mozart: if you will take a *prise*
              or following Ponce ("Ponthe")
                    to the fountain in Florida
de Leon alla fuente florida
              or Anchises that laid hold of her flanks of air
drawing her to him
                         Cythera potens, Κύθηρα δεινά
no cloud, but the crystal body
              the tangent formed in the hand's cup
          as live wind in the beech grove
                    as strong air amid cypress

Κόρη Δῆλια δεινά/ et libidinis expers
the sphere moving crystal, fluid,
          none therein carrying rancour
Death, insanity/suicide degeneration
that is, just getting stupider as they get older
πολλά παθεῖν,

                    nothing matters but the quality
of the affection—
in the end—that has carved the trace in the mind
dove sta memoria

and if theft be the main principle in government
        (every bank of discount J. Adams remarked)
there will be larceny on a minor pattern
a few camions, a stray packet of sugar
        and the effect of the movies
        the guard did not think that the Führer had started it
Sergeant XL thought that excess population
            demanded slaughter at intervals
        (as to the by whom...) Known as 'The ripper.'

    Lay in soft grass by the cliff's edge
with the sea 30 metres below this
            and at hand's span, at cubit's reach moving,
the crystalline, as inverse of water,
        clear over rock-bed

        ac ferae familiares
the gemmed field *a destra* with fawn, with panther,
        corn flower, thistle and sword-flower
        to a half metre grass growth,
lay on the cliff's edge
        ...nor is this yet *atasal*
        nor are here souls, nec personae
        neither here in hypostasis, this land is of Dione
and under her planet
        to Helia the long meadow with poplars
to   Κύπρις
        the mountain and shut garden of pear trees in flower
here rested.

----

    and the spring of their squeak-doll is broken
and Bracken is out and the B.B.C. can lie

but at least a different bilge will come out of it
             at least for a little, as is its nature
can continue, that is, to lie.

             As a lone ant from a broken ant-hill
from the wreckage of Europe, ego scriptor.

spiriti questi? personae?
                    tangibility by no means *atasal*
                    but the crystal can be weighed in the hand
formal and passing within the sphere: Thetis,
Maya, 'Αφροδίτη,

                    no overstroke
             no dolphin faster in moving
                    nor the flying azure of the wing'd fish under
Zoagli
             when he comes out into the air, living arrow.
and the clouds over the Pisan meadows
             are indubitably as fine as any to be seen
from the peninsula
             οἱ βάρβαροι have not destroyed them
             as they have Sigismundo's Temple
    Divae Ixottae (and as to her effigy that was in Pisa?)
    Ladder at swing jump as for a descent from the cross
O white-chested martin, God damn it,
             as no one else will carry a message,
       say to La Cara: amo.
    Her bed-posts are of sapphire
             for this stone giveth sleep.
             and in spite of hoi barbaroi,
             pervenche and a sort of dwarf morning-glory

that knots in the grass, and a sort of buttercup
et sequelae

Le Paradis n'est pas artificiel
    States of mind are inexplicable to us.
     δακρύων   δακρύων   δακρύων
L.   P.   gli onesti
              J'ai eu pitié des autres
probablement pas assez, and at moments that suited my own
    convenience
              Le paradis n'est pas artificiel,
                     l'enfer non plus.
Came Eurus as comforter
and at sunset la pastorella dei suini
    driving the pigs home, benecomata dea

        under the two-winged cloud
        as of less and more than a day
----

woe to them that conquer with armies
    and whose only right is their power.

from CANTO LXXIX

    The moon has a swollen cheek
and when the morning sun lit up the shelves and battalions
of the West, cloud over cloud
              Old Ez folded his blankets
Neither Eos nor Hesperus has suffered wrong at my hands

       O Lynx, wake Silenus and Casey
       shake the castagnettes of the bassarids,

the mountain forest is full of light
             the tree-comb red-gilded
Who sleeps in the field of lynxes
             in the orchard of Maelids?
(with great blue marble eyes
             "because he likes to," the cossak)
Salazar, Scott, Dawley on sick call
             Polk, Tyler, half the presidents and Calhoun
"Retaliate on the capitalists" sd/ Calhoun "of the North"
ah yes, when the ideas were clearer
             debts to people in N. Y. city
             and on the hill of the Maelids
in the close garden of Venus
                    asleep amid serried lynxes
set wreathes on Priapus Ἴακχος, Io! Κύθηρα, Io!
                    having root in the equities
Io!
       and you can make 5000 dollars a year
all you have to do is to make one trip up country
then come back to Shanghai
                    and send in an annual report
as to the number of converts
                    Sweetland on sick call
             ’ελέησον   Kyrie eleison
       each under his fig tree
       or with the smell of fig leaves burning
so shd/ be fire in winter
with fig wood, with cedar, and pine burrs

             O Lynx keep watch on my fire.

164

So Astafieva had conserved the tradition
From Byzance and before then
                    Manitou remember this fire
O lynx, keep the phylloxera from my grape vines

Ἴακχε Ἴακχε, Χαῖρε ΑΟΙ
                    "Eat of it not in the under world"
                    See that the sun or the moon bless thy eating
Κόρη, Κόρη, for the six seeds of an error
or that the stars bless thy eating

              O Lynx, guard this orchard,
              Keep from Demeter's furrow
This fruit has a fire within it,
                    Pomona, Pomona
No glass is clearer than are the globes of this flame
what sea is clearer than the pomegranate body
          holding the flame?
                    Pomona, Pomona,

              Lynx, keep watch on this orchard
              That is named Melagrana
or the Pomegranate field
              The sea is not clearer in azure
              Nor the Heliads bringing light

Here are lynxes   Here are lynxes,
Is there a sound in the forest
                    of pard or of bassarid
or crotale   or of leaves moving?

Cythera, here are lynxes
Will the scrub-oak burst into flower?
    There is a rose vine in this underbrush
Red? white? No, but a colour between them
    When the pomegranate is open and the light falls
half thru it

    Lynx, beware of these vine-thorns
        O Lynx, γλαυκῶπις coming up from the olive yards,

    Kuthera, here are Lynxes and the clicking of crotales
There is a stir of dust from old leaves
    Will you trade roses for acorns
    Will lynxes eat thorn leaves?
What have you in that wine jar?
            ἰχώρ, for lynxes?
Maelid and bassarid among lynxes;
    how many? There are more under the oak trees,
We are here waiting the sun-rise
    and the next sunrise
for three nights amid lynxes. For three nights
    of the oak-wood
and the vines are thick in their branches
    no vine lacking flower,
no lynx lacking a flower rope
    no Maelid minus a wine jar
this forest is named Melagrana

        O lynx, keep the edge on my cider
        Keep it clear without cloud

We have lain here amid kalicanthus and sword-flower
    The heliads are caught in wild rose vine
The smell of pine mingles with rose leaves
            O lynx, be many
            of spotted fur and sharp ears.
            O lynx, have your eyes gone yellow,
            with spotted fur and sharp ears?
Therein is the dance of the bassarids
    Therein are centaurs
And now Priapus with Faunus
    The Graces have brought Ἀφροδίτην
Her cell is drawn by ten leopards
            O lynx, guard my vineyard
            As the grape swells under vine leaf
            Ἥλιος is come to our mountain
            there is a red glow in the carpet of pine spikes

            O lynx, guard my vineyard
            As the grape swells under vine leaf

            This goddess was born of sea-foam
            She is lighter than air under Hesperus
                δεινὰ εἶ, Κύθηρα
terrible in resistance
                Κόρη καὶ Δήλια καὶ Μαῖα
trine as praeludio
                Κύπρις Ἀφρόδιτη
a petal lighter than sea-foam
                Κύθηρα

                    aram
                    nemus
                    vult
                    167

from CANTO LXXX

    Nancy where art thou?
Whither go all the vair and the cisclatons
and the wave pattern runs in the stone
on the high parapet (Excideuil)
Mt Segur and the city of Dioce
Que tous les mois avons nouvelle lune
What the deuce has Herbiet (Christian)
        done with his painting?
Fritz still roaring at treize rue Gay de Lussac
with his stone head still on the balcony?
Orage, Fordie, Crevel too quickly taken

      de mis soledades vengan

lay there till Rossetti found it remaindered
      at about two pence
(Cythera, in the moon's barge whither?
           how hast thou the crescent for car?

or did they fall because of their loose taste in music
      "Here! none of that mathematical music!"
Said the Kommandant when Münch offered Bach to the regi-
                           ment
or Spewcini the all too human
      beloved in the eyetalian peninsula
for quite explicable reasons
    so that even I can now tolerate
    man seht but with the loss of criteria
and the wandering almost-tenor explained to me:

    well, the operas in the usual repertoire
have been sifted out, there's a reason

Les hommes ont je ne sais quelle peur étrange,
        said Monsieur Whoosis, de la beauté

La beauté, "Beauty is difficult, Yeats" said Aubrey Beardsley
    when Yeats asked why he drew horrors
    or at least not Burne-Jones
    and Beardsley knew he was dying and had to
    make his hit quickly

hence no more B-J in his product.

        So very difficult, Yeats, beauty so difficult.

    "I am the torch" wrote Arthur "she saith"
in the moon barge βροδοδάκτυλος Ἠώς

with the veil of faint cloud before her
        Κύθηρα δεινὰ as a leaf borne in the current
pale eyes as if without fire

all that Sandro knew, and Jacopo
        and that Velásquez never suspected
lost in the brown meat of Rembrandt
        and the raw meat of Rubens and Jordaens

"This alone, leather and bones between you and τὸ πᾶν,"
                            [toh pan, the all]
    (Chu Hsi's comment)

Oh to be in England now that Winston's out
    Now that there's room for doubt

And the bank may be the nation's
And the long years of patience
And labour's vacillations
May have let the bacon come home,
        To watch how they'll slip and slide
        watch how they'll try to hide
           the real portent
      To watch a while from the tower
        where dead flies lie thick over the old charter
     forgotten, oh quite forgotten
     but confirming John's first one,
  and still there if you climb over attic rafters;
to look at the fields; are they tilled?
is the old terrace alive as it might be
with a whole colony
         if money be free again?
Chesterton's England of has-been and why-not,
or is it all rust, ruin, death duties and mortgages
and the great carriage yard empty
         and more pictures gone to pay taxes

    When a dog is tall but
    not so tall as all that
    that dog is a Talbot
        (a bit long in the pasterns?)
When a butt is ½ as tall as a whole butt
That butt is a small butt
        Let backe and side go bare
and the old kitchen left as the monks had left it
and the rest as time has cleft it.

[Only shadows enter my tent
                    as men pass between me and the sunset,]
beyond the eastern barbed wire
        a sow with nine boneen
matronly as any duchess at Claridge's

and for that Christmas at Maurie Hewlett's
Going out from Southampton
they passed the car by the dozen
        who would not have shown weight on a scale
                riding, riding
                        for Noel the green holly
        Noel, Noel, the green holly
        A dark night for the holly

That would have been Salisbury plain, and I have not thought
                                                        of
        the Lady Anne for this twelve years
                Nor of Le Portel
How tiny the panelled room where they stabbed him
                In her lap, almost, La Stuarda
        Si tuit li dolh elh planh el marrimen
                for the leopards and broom plants

Tudor indeed is gone and every rose,
Blood-red, blanch-white that in the sunset glows
cries: "Blood,   Blood,   Blood!" against the gothic stone
Of England, as the Howard or Boleyn knows.

Nor seeks the carmine petal to infer;
Nor is the white bud Time's inquisitor
Probing to know if its new-gnarled root
Twists from York's head or belly of Lancaster;

Or if a rational soul should stir, perchance,
Within the stem or summer shoot to advance
Contrition's utmost throw, seeking in thee
But oblivion, not thy forgiveness, FRANCE.

as the young lizard extends his leopard spots
    along the grass-blade seeking the green midge half an ant-
      size
and the Serpentine will look just the same
and the gulls be as neat on the pond
and the sunken garden unchanged
and God knows what else is left of our London
      my London, your London
and if her green elegance
    remains on this side of my rain ditch
      puss lizard will lunch on some other T-bone

sunset grand couturier.

from CANTO LXXXI

Yet
Ere the season died a-cold
Borne upon a zephyr's shoulder
I rose through the aureate sky

> *Lawes and Jenkyns guard thy rest*
> *Dolmetsch ever be thy guest,*

Has he tempered the viol's wood
To enforce both the grave and the acute?
Has he curved us the bowl of the lute?

> *Lawes and Jenkyns guard thy rest*
> *Dolmetsch ever be thy guest*

Hast 'ou fashioned so airy a mood
   To draw up leaf from the root?
Hast 'ou found a cloud so light
   As seemed neither mist nor shade?

> Then resolve me, tell me aright
> If Waller sang or Dowland played.

> Your eyen two wol sleye me sodenly
> I may the beauté of hem nat susteyne

And for 180 years almost nothing.

Ed ascoltando al leggier mormorio
   there came new subtlety of eyes into my tent,
whether of spirit or hypostasis,
   but what the blindfold hides
or at carneval
                   nor any pair showed anger
   Saw but the eyes and stance between the eyes,
colour, diastasis,
   careless or unaware it had not the
   whole tent's room
nor was place for the full image,
interpass, penetrate

casting but shade beyond the other lights
    sky's clear
    night's sea
    green of the mountain pool
    shone from the unmasked eyes in half-mask's space.
What thou lovest well remains,
                  the rest is dross
What thou lov'st well shall not be reft from thee
What thou lov'st well is thy true heritage
Whose world, or mine or theirs
             or is it of none?
First came the seen, then thus the palpable
    Elysium, though it were in the halls of hell,
What thou lovest well is thy true heritage

The ant's a centaur in his dragon world.
Pull down thy vanity, it is not man
Made courage, or made order, or made grace,
    Pull down thy vanity, I say pull down.
Learn of the green world what can be thy place
In scaled invention or true artistry,
Pull down thy vanity,
              Paquin pull down!
The green casque has outdone your elegance.

"Master thyself, then others shall thee beare"
    Pull down thy vanity
Thou art a beaten dog beneath the hail,
A swollen magpie in a fitful sun,
Half black half white
Nor knowst'ou wing from tail

174

Pull down thy vanity
                How mean thy hates
Fostered in falsity,
                Pull down thy vanity,
Rathe to destroy, niggard in charity,
Pull down thy vanity,
                I say pull down.

But to have done instead of not doing
                this is not vanity
To have, with decency, knocked
That a Blunt should open
                To have gathered from the air a live tradition
or from a fine old eye the unconquered flame
This is not vanity.
                Here error is all in the not done,
all in the diffidence that faltered,

from CANTO LXXXIII

\---

as he was standing below the altars
                of the spirits of rain

        "When every hollow is full
                it moves forward"
        to the phantom mountain above the cloud
But in the caged panther's eyes:

                        "Nothing. Nothing that you can do..."

175

green pool, under green of the jungle,
caged: "Nothing, nothing that you can do."

Δρύας, your eyes are like clouds

Nor can who has passed a month in the death cells
     believe in capital punishment
No man who has passed a month in the death cells
     believes in cages for beasts

Δρύας, your eyes are like the clouds over Taishan
     When some of the rain has fallen
       and half remains yet to fall.

The roots go down to the river's edge
     and the hidden city moves upward
       white ivory under the bark

With clouds over Taishan-Chocorua
     when the blackberry ripens
and now the new moon faces Taishan
one must count by the dawn star
     Dryad, thy peace is like water
There is September sun on the pools

Plura diafana
     Heliads lift the mist from the young willows
there is no base seen under Taishan
     but the brightness of 'udor   ὕδωρ
the poplar tips float in brightness
only the stockade posts stand

And now the ants seem to stagger
                as the dawn sun has trapped their shadows,
this breath wholly covers the mountains
            it shines and divides
it nourishes by its rectitude
does no injury
over-standing the earth it fills the nine fields
                to heaven

Boon companion to equity
       it joins with the process
            lacking it, there is inanition

When the equities are gathered together
as birds alighting
it springeth up vital

If deeds be not ensheaved and garnered in the heart
there is inanition

        (have I perchance a debt to a man named Clower)

that he eat of the barley corn
and move with the seed's breath

the sun as a golden eye
            between dark cloud and the mountain

----

    and Brother Wasp is building a very neat house
    of four rooms, one shaped like a squat indian bottle
    La vespa, *la* vespa, mud, swallow system
               177

so that dreaming of Bracelonde and of Perugia
and the great fountain in the Piazza
or of old Bulagaio's cat that with a well timed leap
        could turn the lever-shaped door handle
It comes over me that Mr. Walls must be a ten-strike
with the signorinas
and in the warmth after chill sunrise
an infant, green as new grass,
has stuck its head or tip
out of Madame La Vespa's bottle

mint springs up again
        in spite of Jones' rodents
as had the clover by the gorilla cage
        with a four-leaf

When the mind swings by a grass-blade
        an ant's forefoot shall save you
the clover leaf smells and tastes as its flower.

----

but if Senator Edwards cd/ speak
and have his tropes stay in the memory 40 years, 60 years?
in short / the descent
has not been of advantage either
        to the Senate or to "society"
                        or to the people
        The States have passed thru a
                dam'd supercilious era.
Down, Derry-down /
        Oh let an old man rest.

from CANTO XCI

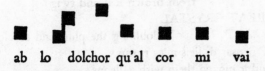

ab lo dolchor qu'al cor mi vai

AB LO DOLCHOR QU'AL COR   MI   VAI

that the body of light come forth
      from the body of fire
And that your eyes come to the surface
      from the deep wherein they were sunken,
Reina—for 300 years,
        and now sunken
That your eyes come forth from their caves
     & light then
            as the holly-leaf
        qui laborat, orat
Thus Undine came to the rock,
               by Circeo
and the stone eyes again looking seaward
    Thus Apollonius
            (if it was Apollonius)
& Helen of Tyre
        by Pithagoras
        by Ocellus
(pilot-fish, et libidinis expers, of Tyre;

179

Justinian, Theodora
                    from brown leaf and twig
The GREAT CRYSTAL
                        doubling the pine, and to cloud.
        pensar di lieis m'es ripaus
Miss Tudor moved them with galleons
from deep eye, versus armada;
in the green deep
                    he saw it,
in the green deep of an eye:
        Crystal waves weaving together toward the gt/
                                healing
Light *compenetrans* of the spirits
The Princess Ra-Set has climbed
            to the great knees of stone,
She enters protection,
            the great cloud is about her,
She has entered the protection of crystal
                    convien che si mova
                    la mente, amando
                            XXVI, 34
Light & the flowing crystal
        never gin in cut glass had such clarity
That Drake saw the splendour and wreckage
        in that clarity
Gods moving in crystal
                    ichor, amor
Secretary of Nature, J. Heydon.

- -

The autumn leaves blow from my hand,
    agitante calescemus . . .
    and the wind cools toward autumn.
Lux in diafana,
           Creatrix,
               oro.
Ursula benedetta,
          oro
By the hours of passion,
              per dilettevole ore,
              guide your successor,
Ysolt, Ydone,
        have compassion,
Picarda,
      compassion
By the wing'd head,
      by the caduceus,
              compassion;
By the horns of Isis-Luna,
              compassion.
The black panther lies under his rose-tree.
J'ai eu pitié des autres.
        Pas assez! Pas assez!
For me nothing. But that the child
    walk in peace in her basilica,
The light there almost solid.

- -

[N.B. USURY (*v.* Canto XLV *et passim*): a charge for the use of purchasing power, levied without regard to production; often without regard even to the possibilities of production. (Hence the failure of the Medici bank.)]

from WOMEN OF TRACHIS

The first KHOROS (accompaniment strings, mainly cellos):

PHOEBUS, Phoebus, ere thou slay   (*Str. 1*)
and lay flaked Night upon her blazing pyre,
Say, ere the last star-shimmer is run:
Where lies Alkmene's son, apart from me?
Aye, thou art keen, as is the lightning blaze,
Land way, sea ways,
in these some slit hath he
found to escape thy scrutiny?

DAYSAIR is left alone,   (*Ant. 1*)
      so sorry a bird,
For whom, afore, so many suitors tried.
And shall I ask what thing is heart's desire,
Or how love fall to sleep with tearless eye,
So worn by fear away, of dangerous road,
A manless bride to mourn in vacant room,
Expecting ever the worse,
       of dooms to come?

NORTH WIND or South, so bloweth tireless   (*Str. 2*)
wave over wave to flood.
Cretan of Cadmus' blood, Orcus' shafts err not.
What home hast 'ou now,
     an some God stir not?

PARDON if I reprove thee, Lady,   (*Ant. 2*)
To save thee false hopes delayed.
Thinkst thou that man who dies,
Shall from King Chronos take
          unvaried happiness?
Nor yet's all pain.

                                   (*drums, quietly added to music*)
The shifty Night delays not,
Nor fates of men, nor yet rich goods and spoil.
Be swift to enjoy, what thou art swift to lose.
Let not the Queen choose despair.
Hath Zeus no eye (who saith it?)
          watching his progeny?

Rural Development: Putting the Last First

Robert Chambers

Longman

London   Lagos   New York

p Limited
ouse
ll, Harlow
CM20 2JE, England
d Associated Companies
throughout the World.

Published in the United States of America
by Longman Inc.

First published 1983
Reprinted 1984

British Library Cataloguing in Publication Data

Chambers, Robert
  Rural development.
  1. Rural pool–Underdeveloped areas
  I. Title
  305.5′69′091724 HC59.7

  ISBN 0-582 64443-7

Library of Congress Cataloging in Publication Data

Chambers, Robert, 1932-
  Rural development.

  Bibliography: p.
  Includes index.
  1. Underdeveloped areas–Rural poor. 2. Rural development.   I. Title.
HN980.C49 1983 307′.14 83-977
ISBN 0-582-64443-7 (pbk.)

Set in 10/11 Melior

Printed in Hong Kong by Wing King Tong Co. Ltd.